Ask Her Out

Pursuing Freedom, Manhood, and Women

Judd Palmer

In *Ask Her Out*, Judd Palmer helps men unravel some of the biggest mysteries they will confront on their relationship journeys. He shares his own story mixed with the powerful revelations he has received. You will be challenged and inspired to change your beliefs about God, yourself, and others as you move forward on the path to healthy mindsets about relationships. Judd, thanks for speaking into this important area of life.

Steve Backlund
Igniting Hope Ministries

For more information,
visit our website:
www.askheroutthebook.com

*I would like to dedicate this book to those who lost their homes
in the Carr Fire
that started in July 2018 and destroyed over eleven hundred
homes and structures.
To the city of Redding, California.*

*Out of the ashes and grief, may beauty and prosperity arise
throughout this land,
in every home and every heart.
Stay strong, stay united.*

Contents

Introduction

On yet another morning spent recovering from overdoing it the night before, I sat on my couch in the large apartment I had all to myself. It was May 14, 2012, and I had recently moved from Portland, Oregon, where I had lots of community. Today, especially, I was feeling the distance from my friends.

That morning, my talk with God went something like this: "Lord, forgive me for sinning last night and for not enjoying life right now. I turn to You and press on and receive Your cleansing." I was recovering from neck surgery following an accident, and in addition to my physical issues, I felt very much alone. It was awful being by myself. In this place it was difficult for me to motivate myself and I knew I was struggling. So, I purposefully praised God for knowing what He was doing, even though I felt incredibly lonely, and I committed my care to Him.

I'm writing this book because I want to talk about being single and how to keep going after that one date didn't work out and—oh, that other one didn't either, and before you know it, you're well into your thirties and saying, "What the heck? What happened?"

I am also writing this book because I have been through pain and regret after crossing the line, and I want to encourage you in overcoming the challenges we face as single men. I want to encourage you into freedom and manhood, to realize how you can contribute to your friends and community, and to see how you can treat women with honor and pursue them with excellence.

This isn't a ten-ways-to-find-the-one book, and I am not the poster child for being single. However, I am learning, growing, and having a good life, and I know what has helped me along the way, so I want to share those things with you.

Thousands of young singles are doing a fantastic job of being happy and having purpose in life. They're doing far better than I did. But there are even more singles who are trying to meet that special someone and are getting frustrated. Some of these guys have anxiety anytime they're around a beautiful woman. They don't get out much and mostly hang out with other guys. For perhaps a variety of reasons, they're single and not enjoying it.

A substantial number of Christian singles feel left out, less than, and passed by. Many of them lack purpose, are depressed or bitter, and don't feel like they have any hope of finding the person who is right for them. Hello to you too. You are welcome here. I speak blessing to your spirit, heart, and mind, and I pray that the truth would rule in your life and decisions and that your heart would expand, so it can receive intimacy with Papa God. I pray that you would be taken to a place of invigorating life, of peace that conquers any situation, where you are filled with courage and, finally, are able to rest in who you are.

And for you females who are reading this book, I hope it helps you and makes a strong impact on your life.

Wherever you are on the single scale, I want to bring encouragement to you. Again, it isn't my goal to get you married but to point you toward health. This book includes much of my story as well as resources, books, teachings, and Scriptures that have been and continue to be part of my story. I want to share what has encouraged and spurred me on to be my best.

Try to apply what I've written here and figure out what works for you. Many, if not all, of the points I make in this book can be applied to any adult situation.

Finally, I am writing this book because people need to get married. Back when my parents were young, it seems like people just got married. It was rare to be thirty and single. But in current American culture, it has become rare to get married young. In certain ways, the world is more complicated than it was in the sixties and seventies.

A shift is needed in our culture—for men to be strong and not held back, for them to pursue women with boldness. And for those pursuits to lead to dating, engagement, and marriage. The purpose of this book is to help you do those things.

I've included an activation section at the end of each chapter. These are designed to help you apply what you've learned and take some kind of action. Hopefully this book will be more than something you just read and think about—maybe it will actually change your life. Dig deep and go for it.

We need to be set free from everything that binds us up and is a barrier to action and health. We need freedom in order to be men. It takes a real man to pursue a woman and to do it well. This book focuses on being healthy and allowing the benefits of that health and strength to lead you to do something important: just asking the woman out.

1
Hey, Man. What's Going On?

When you consider what it means to be a man, what do you think of? What emotions rise within you?

A major reason I am including the subject of manhood in this book is that God made you to be a man, and part of His nature is reflected in your being a man. Life is exhilarating when we thrive in who we were created to be. Being a man allows you to pursue a woman in a healthy and honorable way.

"Being a man" can mean many things to many people. To me, it means being responsible; being truthful; excelling at work; having control over my actions, emotions, and words; facing my fears and overcoming challenges; taking good care of myself in all areas of life; and treating God, others, my possessions, and my country with honor. I could add more to this definition and will attempt to unpack the idea of manhood throughout this book.

When I was younger, particularly in my teen years and into my twenties, I knew I wasn't a man yet. I considered myself a "young man" (which wasn't the same as being a *real* man) or a "guy," but I never thought to myself, *I am a man now.* There was no rite of passage ceremony for me, nor is there for most guys in America.

Now when I consider what it means to be a man, my thoughts turn toward my dad and two older brothers. My dad is a good man, and there are several reasons I think so: He takes responsibility for his actions, he listens well, he engages with others in conversation and doesn't force the conversation to be about him; he is a servant, he knows his weaknesses, he knows how to ask for help, and he loves others well. My dad shows he is a man by facing his fears and the pain from his childhood. He is teachable. He laughs well and often at life, and he is faithful.

But my dad wasn't always this way. When I was growing up, he didn't seem strong to me. And he wasn't. He was passive-aggressive, making little comments about what he wanted or needed or thought other people should do, or blowing up in anger after holding things inside. However, he made a point of spending time with me, and I was able to share with him anything on my mind. To this day, I am very grateful for this. We are good friends and have been for as long as I can remember, and I can honestly say that I really like my dad.

But back when I was in high school, part of me struggled with him. He didn't exude strength or carry himself the way I wanted him to. I thought about my friends' dads and how they were strong and showed their strength even in how they talked, and I wished my dad was more like that.

My dad's dad, my grandfather, was just like that. He was physically strong and talked strong, but he failed to show my dad affection. He never encouraged him.

Which one is more of a man? Is a man someone who is strong physically and tough outwardly? I know that may seem like a dumb question. You may be thinking, *C'mon, Judd. Obviously, a man doesn't have to be physically strong.* Okay, fair enough. But does a "real" man sound tough when you talk to him? Is having confidence what makes a man, a man? Does being a man mean I can't be afraid of anything? Do I become a man only when I am fearless? Or do I become a man when I get married or when I have a good job?

For our purposes in this book, being a man means that you are a male individual (noun) at least eighteen years old who is being a man (verb). *Being a man* is a phrase that describes what you offer the world and other people. It accounts for what you can handle while still maintaining your mental and emotional health. However, it isn't necessarily all encompassing; just because I do something "manly" doesn't mean everything I do is manly or that I am automatically a *good* man.

A man takes responsibility for his own emotions, actions, and belongings and is willing to lay his life down for others. A man is someone who faces his fears and grows continually in health. This means he can look at his fears and still move forward, despite being afraid. Refusing to let fear control him to the point of altering his actions—that is courage.

Fear is needed in this world; there are things we *should* be afraid of. For instance, there is nothing wrong with being afraid of getting hurt. We just don't let that fear freeze us into not moving toward connection with other people.

Being a man means that when I get angry with someone, I take ownership of what I am feeling and don't blame my anger on that person by saying, "This person makes me angry."

1. Hey, Man. What's Going On?

It means that when I make a mistake, I own it and apologize, learn from it, and take steps to make it right, so I won't make that mistake again. If I need help in an area, I go after it. The issue will not go away if I just ignore it.

Being a man means that I honor God with what He has given me—money, a job, my giftings, and belongings—and I am thankful for all these things. It means honoring God by doing everything I do in life unto Him, for His glory.

It means sharing my life with other people and having relationships. I choose to be known instead of isolating or refusing to open up, not connecting, or talking about only those things I am good at or comfortable talking about.

It means laying my life down, thinking of the best interest of others, being unselfish, and being thankful for my friends and family. It means helping those in need, sharing, being there for the people I care about, and being a good listener.

Being a man means seeking help with my issues and not stuffing them inside. In this area of dealing with pain, I didn't always act like a man because I didn't trust God to help me. I didn't step into the pain and process it. There were times when I was able to process my pain in a healthy way, but when I didn't—well, I didn't, and it hurt my relationships in ways I didn't realize at the time. I thought trying to numb my pain, specifically through masturbation, was a personal, private thing that didn't affect my relationships, but as we'll talk about later in the book, it actually prevented me from taking risks with women because I didn't feel strong.

Bringing the Main Dish

Being a man means being able to take advice and be corrected.

I recently planned a family dinner with my new girlfriend at my parents' house. I thought my mom would enjoy making the main dish, and other people could bring side dishes. I was going to bring the salad.

Then my brother called me. "Look," he said. "It isn't right for you to host the family dinner and only bring a salad."

At first I was defensive. "Well," I replied, "it's already planned, and I will think about doing it differently another time. Thanks for telling me." Honestly, I wasn't trying to be lazy. I genuinely thought my mom would want to cook the main meal because that was usually what happened.

But while I was still on the phone, I slowly began to realize my brother was correct and that I had an opportunity to do the right thing, even though I hadn't intended to do the wrong thing. It was in my best interest to heed my brother's advice and provide the main dish. If I chose not to take his advice, I probably wouldn't enjoy the meal as much simply because I wouldn't have been a man about it. Instead, I would be there with my salad and miss out on the greater gift of bringing the main meal.

So, even though I didn't really want to, I went to the grocery store the night before the meal and picked up the biggest roast they had, plus potatoes and carrots, and I put them in the Crockpot the next morning. And everything turned out really well. It was rewarding to provide the main course for my family dinner, something I had never done before, and it was great to show my girlfriend my mean cooking skills.

Had I become defensive and tried to stick up for myself out of insecurity, I would have missed an opportunity to show up, be present, provide for others, offer something valuable, and take a risk. It's always best to listen well to constructive criticism.

My Manstart, You Could Say

I can say with confidence that I am a man. I think I was a man even before this next event occurred, but the story I am about to tell you definitely solidified my belief in this regard, and it also went on to influence my dating life.

When I bought my own business, I felt a real responsibility unlike anything I had carried in the past. I had just come out of grad school (without actually graduating), was hardly making any money, and was just trying to figure out what I wanted to do in life. I asked God for a trade I could enjoy that would give me a decent living, something where I could help people and not add to my school debt.

I ended up training as a hearing aid specialist and took the large state exams for my license. Within six months, I purchased my very own hearing aid practice from a man who wanted to retire, and I became a business owner.

That experience changed my life. When a customer had a question, it was up to me to find the answer. When a customer was upset, it was all on me to find a solution, earn their trust, and keep a good reputation in the small town of Canby, Oregon. I became a man through that experience because of the responsibility put on me and how I handled it.

I didn't know how to own a business or how to operate some of the office equipment. I had to ask questions all the time as I set up the financials and bookkeeping, the credit card machine, the audiometer, the many different hearing aid brands, and all the years of models.

I remember having appointments where I had to call the manufacturer on the spot, asking how to connect to the hearing aid because I had no idea—I was trained only on one brand and my new practice sold about seven brands and over ten years of models. But I made the call, asked the questions, and got the job done.

About two months into it, I hurt my neck while inner tubing on Mount Lassen in Northern California, and I had to keep working because I had no one to cover for me. My injury grew worse and worse until it became horrible trying to sell hearing aids and work with customers when I felt so out of it mentally. The injury affected the nerves going to my brain and caused tingling and numbness in the fingers of my right hand. I even had short-term memory loss to a small degree. Instead of sitting up straight like it was supposed to, my neck jutted forward and to the right.

1. Hey, Man. What's Going On?

But I didn't quit. I kept working. I became a stronger man as I faced those circumstances and the pain and pressed on to do the right thing, no matter what.

Facing Conflict and Fears

For many of us, the principal ingredient of being a man is twofold: overcoming our fears and handling conflict well. Who wants to be a crybaby? Who wants to be pushed around? Who wants to be scared to share his needs with someone else? This double ingredient of facing your fears and handling conflict with others is about being assertive and not passive-aggressive.

This is where dating relationships succeed or fail. This is the key moment.

As you know, conflict can happen in nearly every conversation or interaction, with every type of person. There is a wide range of conflict "types" and different levels on which conflict can occur. But here I specifically want to talk about conflict with people.

When I was a house manager and needed one of the other guys to do the chore assigned to him, I would have to step up and tell him to do it. I didn't *want* to tell him. In fact, I was frustrated that I had to; he should have been doing his chore on his own. I also had concerns about how the conversation would go, but I came at our potentially difficult talk with the belief that it was my role as a house manager to tell him to clean up after himself. I focused on what I was going to say to him and made sure I said it in an honoring tone of voice and didn't make it personal. Meaning, I was not going to judge him as a person by talking in a disrespectful manner. Nor was I going to judge him as less valuable because he hadn't done the chore on his own.

If I had acted according to my feelings in this situation, it is possible that the result would have been the same: He would have finally done the chore. It is also possible that yelling at the guy would have momentarily made me feel good, and it potentially would have created fear in him and motivated him not to be lazy again in the future. While fear can motivate us, and it does work, it is not conducive for building a relationship, and love actually is a better motivator than fear. I chose to show this guy honor and respect, and the outcome was better for both of us.

Another major component of being a healthy man is facing your fears and dealing with them. This will open your mouth when you're talking to a woman you are interested in and allow you to walk across the room with purpose and contentment, even if you are nervous, and start that conversation with her.

The sport teams that work hard and have the most fun together do much better than those that are crippled by the fear of making a mistake and are run by a tyrant coach. And no doubt, you know firsthand that you would rather work with, live with, be in a family with, and be in a relationship with someone who treats you with love instead of threatening you into behavior they approve of.

1. Hey, Man. What's Going On?

Every fear and point of bitterness that I dealt with before talking with my housemate was an opportunity for me to grow, to become stronger in facing those things. I do not like conflict, and there have even been times when I haven't liked myself *because* I was having conflict with someone. That is how much I don't enjoy conflict—to the point of wishing I were different or had different values, just so there wouldn't be conflict. I've had to work hard to train myself in how to face conflict, how to be a good man in spite of conflict, and how to allow God's love to penetrate my scared heart and mind.

In every conflict, interaction, and with every person, we have a choice. Will we be men and reveal Jesus in us to the other person, or will we cave to fear and become passive? Will we be angry and get aggressive? Will we focus on what God thinks about us—or on what others think about us?

As you spend time with God and include Him in every situation in your life, in every area of pain, in your fears, all the unknowns, your dreams and desires, all these things—He will speak to you in your quiet times *and* He will speak to you in times of conflict.

Facing your conflicts with love will lead to peace.

There is no way to have peace without dealing with your conflicts and fears. It is much better to deal with a smaller amount of fear now than it is to let it build up and become a mountain later. In the same way, it's better to work first, just get the job done, and not procrastinate, because this allows you to enjoy your free time without intruding thoughts of all you need to do.

Allowing yourself to become a man will lead you to pursue a woman in a healthy way. You may see plenty of guys who are married or have girlfriends, and they don't seem like "real men" but more like grown children. Those guys aren't you, so we don't need to worry about them. We are focusing on you because you are unique. You are the only you, and you get to be different. In the past I complained about all those lame guys who were with beautiful women—it seems unfair, right? But you are not like them. You don't have to act like a jerk to attract a girl who is interested in jerks. Live as a good man, and a good woman will be attracted to you.

The end goal of freedom isn't to get a girlfriend or wife; it isn't even so you can grow into a great man. The goal of freedom is *freedom*. When you are a truly good man, you get to enjoy it and the reward it brings by positively impacting others.

Activation

We don't practice being men in order to get something in return. True manhood is selfless. Our reward comes from being in relationship with God, from the joy of being selfless and seeing others prosper. We choose to be men for the joy of being able to provide and protect others. For the joy of giving to others, and for the joy of being responsible for our own feelings and actions, not letting someone else dictate how we view ourselves.

1. Hey, Man. What's Going On?

In which areas of your life do you want to grow as a man? What are you willing to face in order to get there? If something is blocking you, what are you going to do about it? Who are you going to talk to for support or encouragement?

One key area that can keep you from maturity is unforgiveness, especially where your father is concerned. If any areas of pain exist between you and your dad, have a talk with him. With gentleness, tell him the areas where he has hurt you and make sure he knows that you forgive him.

If you are unable to talk to him, write a letter expressing the pain and hurt in your relationship or lack thereof. Write out your forgiveness because this will help release you from bitterness, which is painful and prevents you from becoming the man you want to be. After forgiving your dad, burn the letter as an act of conclusion and no longer holding on to it.

Depending on the circumstances of your childhood, you may need to continue forgiving your dad throughout your lifetime as new things come to mind. This may be especially true if you see him often and have an active relationship with him.

Thank God for any areas where your dad was a blessing. Thank Him for how good He is to you and how perfect of a Father He is to you, for how He provides and protects your heart, for His presence and promises.

Finally, thank God for how He is making you into a good father and that you are released from any pain your dad caused you. You are free to be a man of God, reflecting Jesus to everyone in your life.

Single Life Tip

Get a passport and try to fill it up with stamps and visas to as many awesome places as possible. Just do it!

— Chuck

1. Hey Man, What's Going On?

2

Overcoming Disappointment and Using the Weapon of Truth

My birthday party three years ago was a blast. I shared a party with a housemate whose birthday was actually on the same day as mine, and there were lots of people, crazy dancing, and a bonfire in the backyard. I had a great time and felt very thankful.

The next year, my housemate and I decided to have a dress-up party, of all things. It was fun but toward the second half of the evening, I started feeling "single." You probably know what I mean. Even though it was my party, I began to feel a bit depressed and didn't want to be with people anymore, so I left around 10 o'clock, which is unusual for me. My thoughts had unexpectedly taken a more serious turn, and unlike the previous year, I wasn't as thankful to hang out with my friends. Some of my very good friends hadn't been able to make it this time around, and I missed their presence. So, the party ended up kind of being a bummer for me, not a joy.

What do you do when you start feeling disappointed with something? How do you handle disappointment? Whether you're dealing with an event that falls flat or a rejection from a pretty woman, disappointment happens, and it will probably happen again.

What we think about ourselves is a key factor in how we handle disappointment. In order to process disappointment well, we need to have good beliefs about who we are. This keeps us from letting disappointment slowly eat away the great people we are called to be.

Are you able to trust women after one of them breaks your trust? What gets in your way? Will you risk rejection and ask another girl out on a date? Or will you be passive, letting an opportunity slip by because you weren't "feeling" it? Do you easily become jealous and allow that jealousy to turn into bitterness when you see a beautiful woman with someone else?

I've wanted to get married, and was ready to do something about it, since I was twenty-one. At the time of this writing, I am forty-two. I know what loneliness is like. For a time, every Sunday when I was at church and saw the married couples sitting together, my heart would begin to long for my wife, who one day would sit with me in the same way. That sense of disappointment became real again. A deep feeling of lack was right there beside me.

Then when Thanksgiving, Christmas, Easter, and my birthday came around—man, I've experienced so many special events and occasions where I had a good time, but I also felt sad because I didn't have my wife and children to enjoy them with me.

What are you supposed to do when you feel this way?

Should I Listen to My Thoughts and Emotions?

In this brief discussion of emotions, I want to be careful. Is it normal to feel disappointed or potentially discouraged when you're waiting for something to happen? Of course. But our emotions can end up controlling us if we allow them to. This occurs because our emotions often arise from what we believe about something, usually ourselves.

If I allow my beliefs about myself that are lies to be stronger than my beliefs about myself that are true, it changes how I feel about my circumstances and also what I do about those circumstances. The night of my birthday party, I started thinking, *I don't belong here. Most of these people are way younger than me. Great. Another party being single*. Blah blah blah.

This same thoughts-causing-emotions principle applies to work and looking for a job. When I moved to Redding, California, I got a job working for an insurance agent. I changed careers just so I could move to that city. I'd been a hearing aid specialist for seven years by that point, and since I couldn't find a job in that field, even after looking for quite some time, I decided I would try something different that could still help people and possibly pay more.

As I began studying for my insurance license, I realized I didn't find insurance very interesting, but I stuck it out anyway.

Declarations vs. Vows

During this time, I began to religiously study Steve Backlund's book *Declarations: Unlocking Your Future*, which continues to be a tremendous benefit to me. In this book he includes a challenge to write one hundred declarations and repeat them every day.[1]

A declaration is a statement of something that is true or that we want to be true. Making a vow such as "I will never be hurt again" doesn't really help me. A vow to protect myself from getting hurt will end up damaging me in the long run because it can lead me away from having friends and being in a relationship. If I want to avoid being hurt again, the best way I can do that is by staying away from people and not allowing anyone to get close to me. A vow in this context is like a wall you build around yourself. The more you focus on the wall, the higher and wider it grows. It would be better for me to make a declaration instead that says, "I am loved perfectly by God, and what He thinks about me matters, not what others think."

Here is another example of a destructive vow: "I will never be like my dad." If I embrace that statement, I am actually focusing on my dad and the pain he caused me, and slowly I will start behaving more and more like him because his behavior is what I am focusing on. It eventually becomes routine for me. In a similar way, if I believe I won't be successful, and I tell myself so

---

[1] Steve Backlund et al., *Declarations: Unlocking Your Future* (Redding, CA: Igniting Hope Ministries, 2013).

over and over again, I will—by faith—do things that thwart my success.

But declarations, on the other hand, are positive statements that bring life. The Bible offers several reasons for declarations and why they work:

- "The tongue can bring death or life; those who love to talk will reap the consequences" (Prov. 18:21).
- "Anxiety in the heart of man causes depression, but a good word makes it glad" (Prov. 12:25 NKJV).
- "So then faith comes by hearing, and hearing by the word of God" (Rom. 10:17 NKJV).
- "Let the weak say, 'I am strong'" (Joel 3:10 NKJV).

As I prepared to move to Redding, the declarations I've included in this chapter were invaluable to me. I would repeat them to myself while I was studying and taking exams to be an insurance agent, a job I ended up quitting one month later because it wasn't a good fit for me. I found no reward in it and didn't want my boss to pay for my training when I knew I wasn't going to be there very long. I stepped away from that job before having another job lined up, which is not what I recommend doing, but I sensed strongly that it was the right thing for me and knew I was acting with integrity toward my boss. That was a Friday, and a job opened up on Monday for a hearing aid specialist.

2. Overcoming Disappointment and Using the Weapon of Truth

The Power of Declarations

Here are a few examples of what Scripture-based declarations can look like. When Steve Backlund addresses peace in his book, he bases the following declarations on John 14:27[2] and Isaiah 26:3.[3]

1. I speak to any worry, stress, or anxiety, and I say you cannot stay. Peace reigns in this temple.
2. Because I trust in God, I am kept in perfect peace.
3. I am known as a peace carrier at home, in the workplace, and in all areas of my life.
4. I have a unique ability to remain peaceful, even as responsibilities increase.[4]

Here are a few of my own declarations, which I read aloud every day:

1. I will make good decisions today.
2. God's presence is with me.
3. My peace comes from being in God's presence.
4. I rest in God's beautiful and wonderful ways.
5. I am strengthened by His presence.
6. I am loved perfectly.
7. I have favor with God.
8. The joy of the Lord is my strength.
9. I will do well at any job I do.

---

[2] "Peace I leave with you, My peace I give to you" (NKJV).

[3] "You will keep in perfect peace all who trust in you."

[4] Backlund et al., *Declarations*, 30.

10. I have wisdom to say the right things and to do the right things.
11. I am powerful because You are in me!
12. There is a wife for me!
13. You do know how to give me good gifts.
14. I am a blessing to my family.
15. I am a good steward of my money and finances.
16. I will make enough to cover my bills and have excess beyond my ways!
17. I laugh at the lies of the enemy!
18. I do not have to strive after anything. Everything comes to me.
19. My joy is in the Lord!
20. I laugh at the lie that I am missing out on anything!
21. I am filled with peace that surpasses my understanding.
22. I delight in God's presence!
23. I can do all things through You.
24. No one has to like me and I do not have to strive to please anyone.
25. I am loved so much that I am protected and do not need to put up a wall to protect myself.
26. I do not need to strive after anything because the impossible happens by rest and trust.

These declarations are meant to bring glory to God, not to get selfish gain. They are never meant to override God's purposes. We have a combination of free will and God's plan for us, and this means we are required to take action. If I sit on the couch all day, I won't get anything done. I can declare many things while sitting on the couch, but if I don't actually *do* something, nothing is guaranteed to happen. I am not trying to override God's sovereignty by having faith in His goodness and declaring truth and Scriptures; instead, these things encourage me and I am able to move boldly. This is called partnering with God.[5]

Believing that God is good and declaring His truth were powerful acts for me when I was struggling to adjust to life in my new city. I didn't ignore my circumstances or deny the facts, but I pressed into God and did my part. I looked for work again—and a job came up. I don't mean to suggest that this is a "formula" for success, but it is what God did in my life.

When I was single, I declared that I would meet my wife and get married—because I wanted those two things. I would make other declarations every day as well. I did this because I wanted to be hopeful. I wanted to be attractive to my future wife when I finally met her. No one is attracted to a hopeless person, except maybe another hopeless person. So I tried to keep my heart in good shape by thanking God for my future wife and that He is good no matter what. I thanked Him for filling me with His love and presence and for comforting me. I also thanked Him for using my singleness for good. Hope helps you have a good life, stay encouraged, be joyful, and even love other people.

Honestly, which is better: to have faith and boldly believe what God says or to stay right where we are—bogged down beneath

---

[5] For more information about declarations, I highly recommend *Declarations: Unlocking Your Future* by Steve Backlund (Igniting Hope Ministries, 2013).

the lie that we're messed up? So many of us feel like we don't have anything to offer someone, that we've sinned too much to deserve a wife, that we're bad people or not man enough, that we're too shy or too aggressive, that we're not smart or good looking enough, that we're too rough or not good communicators, that we don't have enough money to support someone, and so forth. Unfortunately, many of us choose the lies.

I would rather believe and hope in God and align myself with truth. It makes my days so much more enjoyable.

Activation

Perhaps you don't have a lot of money right now. That's a fact, not a lie. But the truth is more powerful and it boldly declares, "God is my provider and I will trust Him. I can meet a nice girl regardless of how much money I have. I will do my best to work hard and commit everything I do to Him. I will give my tithe and I will be generous, not stingy. I will be a good steward of what I have. My value is not in how much money I have but in being loved by God."[6]

There are so many aspects to dealing with disappointment that I can't include them all in this book if I want to discuss other topics as well. I don't want this chapter to come across like, "Just get over it and think positively." Honestly, I care about your disappointments, and I want you to know that what you

---

[6] This is based on Romans 8:31–39.

are going through matters. It is important. I hope you have friends and family to talk about how you are doing on a daily basis.

But it is time to start believing the truth.

Pray this prayer as often as necessary:

> *God, thank You for Your tender heart toward me. Thank You that You are victorious in all things and that You are good. Though I don't understand why I am still single, and there are times when it is painful and disappointing, this doesn't take away from Your goodness, for that is who You are: You are good. I give You my disappointments and release them to You. I don't want to carry that load anymore. I receive Your truth, Your Word, Your hope, Your provision, Your kindness, Your goodness, Your favor, and every other spiritual blessing. I trust You to bring me my wife, and I trust You to help me be a good man during the friendship, dating, and engagement period. I seek You first and want Your kingdom to come and Your will to be done in my life as it is in heaven. All of this is for Your glory, God. You know how to give me good gifts because You are a good Father. I align my spirit, heart, and mind with Your will and goodness. Open my eyes to see opportunity, to bless others, to be a good friend, to honor*

women, and to see and treat them the way You
do, because they are Your daughters.

Single Life Tip

Remind God of the desires of your heart and live each day with zest. At forty, it's been worth the wait. The man I'm with now has eclipsed all the ones before. God knows what He's doing! And I'm ten times the woman I was ten years ago! You, my friend, have good coming.

— Deborah

2. Overcoming Disappointment and Using the Weapon of Truth

3

The Highway of Honor Is Smooth

One time I went on a walk with a friend, and I wasn't sure how much I was interested in her. This was our second time hanging out, and though I already knew I wasn't attracted to her as much as I hoped or actually needed to be, I wanted to give it another chance. On our first outing together, we went out for coffee and had a good time. So I thought our walk would go well too.

But it was just okay. The more we talked, the more obvious it became that we had some things in common but not enough, and I realized we wouldn't ever be anything more than friends. She was an amazing woman who knew how to be a great support, which is vital for any friendship; she was sweet and kind and a good listener, among many other things. I just didn't feel like we were a good match.

As I was driving home, I felt bummed that I wasn't more interested in her. Do you ever think that way? I wanted to be in a relationship, but that meant I actually needed to *like* someone.

This stinks, I thought and suddenly found myself dealing with a bunch of emotions I didn't want: disappointment, feeling like a victim, feeling stuck, even self-loathing.

But then another thought occurred to me, and I grabbed hold of it: *No, there is someone out there I am interested in. It's okay that I'm not interested in this other person romantically. I will believe truth so that I stay hopeful. I will rest in God's perfect love for me.*

Honoring Myself and Others

To walk in a healthy way through my single years, I had to honor myself, God, the women I was dating or getting to know, and the other people around me. Honor allows me to love and accept myself even when I don't have everything I want. When disappointment wants me to reject myself because of a perceived failing (many people consider being single a "failing"), I get to honor myself instead. Honor allows me to love myself the way God does. Like many men, I have struggled most of my life to love myself, but through personal experience, I can say with certainty that it is possible to see amazing growth in this area.

The concept of honor spreads to cover many areas we wouldn't necessarily expect. For instance, we can honor even the process of dating and getting to know someone. How do you honor a *process*? By being thankful for it. You get to thank God that you are friends with this woman, that He made you who you are, and that He made her who she is. Being grateful causes honor.

I used to think I was "owed" a relationship, that I deserved to be in one. I thought I was entitled to marriage, to have my dates work out, and to see things progress. "This woman should like me because I am *so great*."

Entitlement is controlling and yucky, isn't it?

I would often get frustrated at myself for not being with someone or for yet another date not working out. It was like I thought that getting mad at myself would somehow motivate me to become "better." But that isn't how we were made to respond.

If we want someone to perform well at their job, we don't treat them harshly. We treat them well. Because I treat my secretary with respect and value her, she works hard for me and cares about respecting me in return. If I talked down to her for forgetting to do something, she wouldn't feel as inspired to work hard for me. Then I wouldn't enjoy working with her as much, and things would continue to go down hill. Even if I need to ask her to change the way she does something, I can do this with honor and not in a way that judges her as a person.

This approach gets much better results than suggesting to her with my body language or words, "You are less of a person because you made this mistake." Encouraging her or saying thank you on a regular basis creates a positive work environment. (I know that probably sounds cliché, but it's true.)

In the same way, when I feel like a failure because I didn't get that second date, or perhaps don't want the second date, it is important for me to "talk nice" to myself. I can still represent Jesus in me. I can live life without falling into a depression and taking days to recuperate. I can grieve and be down and frustrated for a little while, but I can get over it and move on.

When I kick myself for not performing well or not having what I want, I actually won't perform well for a while. I won't think highly of myself because I've been telling my soul that I'm messed up, too picky or too sensitive, not cool enough, too shy or too bold, that I'm expecting too much, or whatever that date felt like to me.

Why do we treat ourselves badly when we feel rejected? This usually occurs because we've set ourselves up as judge. We feel bad about what happened, so we blame ourselves and feel a need to express our judgment.

I am terrible at judging myself because I am a hard taskmaster. Just as we are to consider ourselves with a sober mind (Rom. 12:3), not thinking too highly of ourselves, it is good not to think too lowly either. I honor myself as I speak with grace to my heart and not judge with harshness. This makes for a smooth drive instead of a rocky crash-and-bang with potholes.

The Benefits of Honoring Others

Last year I went on a blind date set up by an acquaintance. We met at a cool restaurant and right away I realized we weren't a good match. Though we had a fairly interesting conversation, we weren't connecting well and the date ended up feeling rather cordial.

No matter who is sitting across from you, honoring that person is the best way to go. I wanted to honor this woman first of all because she was created in God's image. But I also honored her because I wished to honor the acquaintance who set us up; this was his idea, so I wanted to treat this woman well. I honored her in part because I am a gentleman, and by honoring her, I was actually honoring myself. Finally, I honored her because our blind date is part of her story. I wanted to treat her as well as I could so she would have a good time, be blessed, and feel special, even though we would never see each other again. At least, not in a dating situation.

Just as we honor our parents simply because they are our parents (Ex. 20:12), we honor others simply because God made them—because they are loved just as much as we are loved. Even though they may not end up being "the one" for us or they don't act the way we were hoping they would, we can choose to honor them.

Honor is defined as a privilege; it means to have high respect and to esteem someone or something. We say, "It is an honor to be with you," or "It is an honor to serve you." At work I try to honor every customer who walks in the door and every person I speak with on the phone but, as you'll see in my next story, honor isn't always easy.

One time I tested a customer's hearing and fit her for hearing aids. The appointment went well, or so I thought, but when she returned with her husband for the follow-up appointment, she was highly critical of me. Surprised, I had a hard time just accepting her complaints and moving on. I made adjustments to her hearing aids, and it was clear that she appreciated how I helped her.

But then a few days later, she called and said she wanted to return the hearing aids and go somewhere else. And she wouldn't tell me the reason. I pride myself on having nearly zero returns in a year. In fact, that was only the second return I had that entire year. When she came to the office to return them, I asked again what had happened and she completely dismissed me.

"If you want to know why I'm returning them," she said, "you can find out from the insurance company."

At that point, I had been a hearing aid specialist for eight years. I am nationally board certified and I know what I'm doing. I care about having the best fit for my customers, not just what the computer program recommends or what seems like a good idea in the moment.

You know how two doctors can have the same degree, but one of the doctors is helpful and the other makes poor recommendations or just isn't a good listener? So it is with hearing aid specialists. With every customer, I work hard to put myself in that first category.

I did my best with this woman, which meant I acted respectfully toward her. Did I do anything wrong? Nope. Did I need to defend myself? No, it was just her decision. She was difficult to work with, and I found out when I called the insurance company that they'd had a difficult time working with her as well.

But here's my point: By staying in control of my emotions and continuing to treat her well, even though she spoke to me in a demeaning tone of voice and wouldn't explain why she was returning the products, I was able to represent myself accurately. In a way, even though I lost a customer, I was still able to call the situation a win because I won the battle for my attitude. She was trying to make me feel bad, and though I certainly didn't feel *good*, I acted with honor and respect.

In Your Best Interest. Really.

Years ago I served as a group facilitator for ARMS—Abuse Recovery Ministry and Services in the Portland, Oregon, area. I worked with abusive men, some of whom were court ordered to take these classes for one year, while others were there because they were "wife ordered."

One of the biggest themes of the class was being Christlike. An example was honoring your wife, girlfriend, or children when they weren't treating you as you thought they should be. These men were taught to take responsibility for themselves, for their own attitude and actions, and not blame their actions on their family members. They learned to humble themselves and honor their families as Christ honors all of us and laid down His life for us.[7]

It's easy to honor someone when they treat you well or when you think they deserve your honor. But it's a whole other ballgame when someone hurts you, demeans you, ignores you, or disrespects you.

---

[7] *Discovering the Mind of a Woman* by Ken Nair was required reading for the ARMS men's group. I've read this book somewhere around five times because I want the reminders. I highly recommend it.

3. The Highway of Honor Is Smooth

It really is in our best interest to honor the people around us. Jesus instructed us to bless and pray for our enemies. When we honor and bless the people who attack or reject us, we are no longer under their influence and we are free to move on. There is a shift in the spirit realm. It is difficult for our enemies to keep attacking us if we are no longer smitten by their smite.

Many times someone's aggressive actions meant to cause pain can actually turn out for our good. It is also possible for that person to morph into a friend one day, and the turnaround can be miraculous, if not beautiful.

It's also in our best interest to honor others because it shows honor toward our Creator. It shows honor toward life in general, which in turn honors us.

In 1 Peter 3:7, we as men are called to honor our wives and live in an understanding way, so that our prayers are not hindered (TPT):

> Husbands, you in turn must treat your wives with tenderness, viewing them as feminine partners who deserve to be honored, for they are co-heirs with you of the "divine grace of life," so that nothing will hinder your prayers.

Honoring someone means I withhold my judgment. Though I may not understand, I climb to the same level as that person and I ask questions. I seek understanding.

When you're on a date—especially when you're on a *challenging* date—remember that this woman is someone's future wife. You bless her along the way and treat her as if she were Jesus. If you do these things, no matter what happens, the date will end well for you.

Standing Ovation

On a Sunday at church earlier this past year, we honored our veterans. Standing to our feet, we praised them and showed them how we felt about their sacrifices for our country. Later in the service, the pastor spoke about a family serving in Tibet as missionaries, and we honored them as well. Honoring others adds value to life and keeps the value of life strong. It was a privilege for *me* to honor this family, whose members are doing amazing things over there in Tibet. It was a benefit for *me* to thank veterans for all they have sacrificed for us, for our country.

When you are with a woman, show her honor because it is a privilege to be with her. I'm not saying you have to be serious and somber about it; I'm saying it's in your best interest to approach her with this simple mindset: "It is a privilege to be with this woman." She is a beauty to unveil.

In their book *Captivating,* John and Stasi Eldredge write:

> Woman is the crown of creation—the most intricate, dazzling creature on earth. She has a crucial role to play, a destiny of her own. And she, too, bears the image of God (Gen. 1:26), but in a way that only the feminine can speak . .

. When you are with a woman, ask yourself,
"What is she telling me about God?" It will open
up wonders for you.[8]

John writes in *Wild at Heart*:

The reason a woman wants a beauty to unveil,
the reason she asks, *Do you delight in me?* is
simply that God does as well. God is captivating
beauty. As David prays, "One thing I ask of the
Lord, this is what I seek . . . that I may . . . gaze
upon the beauty of the Lord" (Ps. 27:4). Can
there be any doubt that God wants to be
worshipped? That he wants to be seen, and for
us to be captivated by what we see?[9]

Activation

Pray the following prayer:

*God, I turn away from trying to judge myself
and let You be the Judge instead. I turn away
from talking down to myself, punishing myself,
or striving in my own strength to be a better
person. Thank You for making me the way You
did, and thank You for Your gift of grace that*

[8] John and Stasi Eldredge, *Captivating: Unveiling the Mystery of a Woman's Soul* (Nashville: Thomas Nelson, 2005), 27.
[9] John Eldredge, *Wild at Heart: Discovering the Secret of a Man's Soul* (Nashville: Thomas Nelson, 2001), 38.

*allows me to love myself the way You do. I need
Your help to do this, and I receive Your power,
love, and truth. I forgive myself because You
have forgiven me. I agree with You, God.*

*Lord, help me to see people, including myself,
the way You do. Help me to honor everyone and
even the journey I am on. I know I honor You by
honoring myself and others.*

I bless your spirit with honor toward others, yourself, and God. I bless your dates to be filled with honor. I bless all your communication with women to be filled with honor, as well as all your interactions at work and with family.

No matter how someone treats you, may you be able to show honor in return. Be a man by showing honor.

3. The Highway of Honor Is Smooth

Single Life Tip

My verse for interacting with men has always been "Now that you have purified yourselves by obeying the truth so that you have sincere love for your brothers, love one another deeply from the heart" (1 Pet. 1:22). Lately I've been asking myself, "What would it take for ____ (whoever I'm spending time with that day) to be a better man because he has known me?" I've by no means figured it out, but it is a fun place to experiment.

— Christina

4
Workin' It

I started working in fifth grade. I collected newspapers to turn in for recycling. (This was back when they paid you to collect them.) Filling up the trunk and the whole back seat, we would drop the papers off when we had a full load. I also picked berries at the orchards and one day made an amazing twenty bucks. I chopped wood and mowed the lawn for the elderly woman across the street.

My parents wanted me to learn how to be responsible and work hard. Throughout my childhood, I always paid for my own clothes, with the exception of my shoes. Several decades later, this work ethic stays with me.

Being able to provide for yourself can indicate how you will provide for a wife. A responsible man is attractive to a woman. Your work can reflect your endurance and strength as well as your commitment and dedication to that commitment. It shows a woman what you are doing with your life, what you're involved in, how hard you've worked in the past, the hardships you've conquered, a transition you may be in, and what you are passionate about. Work is important, but at the same time, your work does not define you. It does not represent the full scope of who you are.

I want to talk about work in this book because it is an important topic for us as men, and it can impact our dating mojo. Though this will be a good review no matter your age, this chapter is geared mostly toward younger men who may still be figuring out what they think about life, work, being a provider, etc. I want to pass on to you some of the wisdom I've gained over the years.

One of the first things I want to address is the importance of following your desires where work is concerned. Do what you want to do and the money will follow. Do what you have to do and you will survive. There is a time to survive and a time to *thrive*.

If you're in a "surviving" period, if you really need a job and time is running out, get what you can get. If you don't have savings and you need money ASAP, do whatever it takes. Ask friends, post on social media, do odd jobs, get a temp job, and don't spend money on "extra" things like going to the movies, dates, or eating out. For a season, you might need to stick to "beans and rice and Jesus Christ!"

But if you're doing a job you don't like or don't get much reward out of, don't assume you'll be stuck at this job for years to come. Take care of what you need to take care of, and the things you want to do will happen eventually.

As you work that less-than-desirable job, spend your free time getting your resume ready and looking for more desirable work. Or go to school and develop an interesting skill or qualification. A degree of any kind still helps. And take care of yourself. Stay in community and hang out with your friends. Don't hide away because you don't like your job or you feel like you don't have anything to offer.

Finally, if you're broke, keep going. As you take care of your bills on time—things like rent, credit cards, insurance, and continuing to tithe—you will protect yourself from worse financial disaster. Remember, your "survival job" doesn't define you nor does it label your skill set and desire. In time, as you get caught up and look for a better job, you will get to see your goals come together, and you will be able to have the fun adventures you have wanted to have.

Dating When You're Broke

Don't shy away from girls if you don't have money. You can still get to know a woman without spending money.

What things could you do for free, just to hang out with her? Here are a few ideas: Go for a walk, have a picnic, hang out at your house with other people, hang out at her place with other people, cook food together instead of eating at a restaurant. When you do things with a woman that don't entail spending money, you communicate that you are interested in her and enjoy her company enough that you're happy just being with her. Living within your means, and not using a credit card just to impress her, shows character—and that, my friend, is attractive. That you are confident enough to do simple things with her means a lot because it is the thought that counts, especially in this inning.

Down the road when you have more money, take her to a nice place and show her a good time. But don't try to impress her when you can't afford it. Why? Because when you don't have money for basic and essential things like a car payment, gas, food, rent, and your bills, then who cares that you took a girl to a nice restaurant or on a trip? You can't keep your car because you didn't make the car payment, or you don't have enough money for groceries because you overspent.

Suck It Up

In 2006 I had a good job as a production planner and purchaser for a large steel manufacturer that made airplane parts, medical parts, and land-based engines. It paid well, but it was stressful. The stress became much worse when I also "acquired" the title of senior accounting clerk, something I didn't enjoy at all. I made good money, received bonuses, and could access lots of overtime if I wanted it. This job helped me pay off $13,000 in credit card debt in two years.

But my heart wasn't in it. I didn't care about airplane engine parts; I wanted to help people. So I ended up quitting and becoming a caregiver. I also volunteered at church and enrolled in graduate school in the counseling program.

After three semesters of school, one day I was goofing around on the steep hills of the Oregon coast and injured myself. Everything going on in my life—school, work, and volunteering—came to a halt. I was in so much pain that I couldn't do anything for several weeks. It was a low-back injury that pinched the nerves leading to my testicles, which made them feel like they were being squeezed. Very painful.

During this time of forced rest, I had plenty of opportunities to think about what I wanted to do in life (again). It's amazing what pain can do to us, how it can bring out the best in us and highlight the desires that may not have been recognizable until that moment. I realized I didn't want to become a professional counselor and I didn't want to accrue more school debt. Instead, I wanted to do something that would help people, make good money, not require years of additional schooling, have some technical aspects, and be interesting.

So, as I told you earlier, when an opportunity came up for me to be trained as a hearing aid specialist, it seemed to be a good fit for me. Six months after obtaining my license, I purchased a small practice just south of Portland and became a business owner. Nine years later, I am still in this rewarding career.

I never thought I would be a hearing aid specialist. It was completely not on my radar. It does, however, include many things that I enjoy doing. After working dozens of jobs prior to this, I finally found a trade that I enjoy, one about which I can say, "Wow—I get paid to help people hear better!"

It is important to go after what you want to do. You may not know the exact job right now, but you can find out the *themes* that excite you or are rewarding for you.

When you talk to a woman about your job, what you want to do, or what you are studying, be yourself and be honest about your position. What you are currently doing for work may represent where you are in life, but again, it may not. So don't worry about it. The main thing is to work for the Lord, because

4. Workin' It

He sees everything you do and will reward you. A reward can come in many forms. It could be a sense of accomplishment for doing good work even if you didn't need to. It could look like having internal peace because you treated customers like they were Jesus, as we are called to do (Matt. 25:40). It could look like building patience and character, or it could even look like getting promoted. This may be a job that leads to another job.

But whatever this job leads to, it will work out for your good. God doesn't waste anything.

You are a citizen of heaven. When you're working for the Lord, your work is as worship unto Him (Col. 3:23). If that sounds crazy to you, try it for a time and then form your opinion. I tell you what—it will be much more enjoyable for you to work for the Lord than to complain and look at your job through critical eyes. I know because I've been there. I've had some horrible jobs, but I tried to make the best of them.

I once had a survival job working at one of those kiosks in a shopping mall. You know the ones—they have cool things for sale like trinkets that fly and remote-controlled trucks, or there's the less cool version that sells cell phones or portable steam irons. Then there was me, working at a kiosk for a trade school. Yes, it was as boring and lame as it sounds. I would just stand there smiling at shoppers as they walked by. I wasn't selling anything and had a form for people to fill out if they wanted information about the school. That was it. For hours and hours and hours. When a former high school classmate saw me, I was humiliated. Yep, that's what I was doing after all these years—working for a temp company at a kiosk for a trade school. I tried to make the best of it by having a good attitude and smiling at people.

Become a thermostat, not a thermometer. Change the "temperature" instead of just reflecting what's going on around you. With an unjust boss or supervisor, work for the Lord and bless that person; pray for them. Pray for your customers and coworkers. The only thing you can control in this situation is yourself. So shine and leave behind the whine.

If you choose not to work for the Lord, the alternative isn't very pleasant. It probably means being depressed, hating your job, and being unable to stand what's happening to you. It means not having money and maybe not having a job at all. It probably means going into debt too.

Even if your job sucks, you can respect your boss and show your customers or clients honor. You can work hard and gain favor.

Instructions Not Included

If you have a job you like, awesome. Commit everything you do to the Lord. Ask the Holy Spirit to give you wisdom as you work and do what He shows you. You might be surprised at how fun this is. As He gives you ideas, you get to do them and totally rock.

Keep dreaming. Look at what you like to do, at where your heart is, and commit your dream to the Lord. Go to those who are currently doing what you want to do, and ask them how they got there.

One key to being successful is always asking questions and being teachable. It doesn't matter how little you know right now; if you have the courage to ask questions, you will continue to learn. There is no condemnation for not knowing something, but there is stupidity in doing nothing because you don't know the answer. You have the opportunity to be a man or to be passive. So make the better choice. Choose to be a man, ask questions, and be open to growing and learning.

You might feel like asking questions makes you come across as weak and vulnerable, but you are actually showing strength because you're focusing on growing and you care about doing a good job. It's better to be vulnerable and ask questions than to cower in shame and not do what you want to do. Be the guy who stops and asks for directions.

What Do You Really, Really Want?

If you have a pretty good idea of what you want to do in life, take a few minutes and tell yourself why you think you would be good at that particular job. How you talk about it and how it makes you feel will help you discover how confident you are in this decision. Do you get nervous and shaky when talking about it? Or does it light a fire in you?

If you're unsure what you want to do, ask your close friends or family a couple of simple questions: "What do you think I would like to do? Do you think I would be good at that?"

If you're like a lot of other people, you may have a tendency to try to analyze everything and come up with the perfect "you," only to find out later that it wasn't a good fit. Don't try to figure yourself out by yourself. Chances of success are higher if you include other people in your decision, because they can act as sounding boards and bounce feedback to you.

At times, trying to figure out your career is like over analyzing a girl before you even ask her out. You could analyze yourself right out of it, thinking she would never say yes, but until you actually start talking with her, you miss out on the experience of being with her. Trying to figure out your career can be like that. Yes, there are the careers you know you don't want to pursue, but for those you think you *could* like, start knocking on doors and see which ones open.

What does it mean to knock on doors in this context? It depends on where you live, who you know, what you know, and what kind of job you are looking for.

If you have questions about your career, I recommend the book *What Color Is Your Parachute?* by Richard N. Bolles.[10] I've actually read several editions of this book because economies change, job markets change, and I have changed. This book will

---

[10] Emeryville, CA: Ten Speed Press.

help you discover what you want to do in life—and a whole lot more.

If you aren't working right now, then spend eight hours a day looking for work. That's your job right now. Search online at job board sites, apply to multiple places and for multiple positions, and create a few different resumes that you can easily tailor to fit each job opening. (For example, keep the job experience and profile the same but change the objective.)

Write a cover letter that clearly states why you are a good fit for this specific job, what attracts you to it, and how your past experience or education qualifies you for it. Feel free to contact certain companies and give them your resume, even if they say they aren't hiring. Their plans could change, and they may create a job for you or something could open up.

Ask your friends or family if they know a place that is hiring. Ask God where to look. Ask for help.

As you try to determine the career you want, write out what you would like in the ideal job and the things you wouldn't like. Realize that you probably won't have 100 percent of the things you like—and that's okay. You may like only 85 percent of what a specific job offers, and that's actually a high percentage, especially when you consider all the people who don't like their jobs at all. Don't settle, but don't discount a career because it's not 100 percent of your wish list.

Finally, if you are getting bored with your career, find someone who has a better job than you do or who is more successful. Spend time with them and be challenged to grow. If you don't know someone who has more influence than you do, ask God to bring that person to you.

The opposite of growth is stagnation. It is lame to be stagnant because it means that you are not as alive as you could be. Criticism, pride, and all sorts of negative things can start happening when a person is "stagnant."

Ask Not What Your Community Can Do for You

Don't be just a consumer. Instead, give of yourself and make a difference. It is super rewarding to volunteer and give of your time and resources to others, and it can also help you appreciate the job you actually get paid to do.

Doing something for free can be fun because it stretches you and helps you realize that life isn't all about making money. Volunteering develops your heart, teaches you to enjoy new things, and allows you to get a taste of other types of activities. It could even lead to a career change, and it makes a difference in others' lives and improves your community.

Take ownership of your community by serving. Don't just *pray* for change; be the change.

I volunteer as a greeter for the first service at my church. I get to open the doors, greet people, and wish them a good morning. I also volunteer in the healing rooms and on the ministry team; I love doing these things and being part of something larger than myself. If you could volunteer anywhere, what would you want to do? Where would you want to help out?

Volunteering is an excellent way to meet friends and build community. When you take the time to serve alongside others, it builds a strong bond within your team.

There have been seasons when I didn't volunteer very much and other seasons when I did much more. Do what you want to do and commit yourself to the task at hand, but also feel free to back out of something if you need time for another priority. Make sure you are taking care of yourself. There are endless ways to volunteer, and you'll quickly discover that everyone wants your time, so in addition to its other benefits, volunteering becomes a good way to practice saying no.

When you don't have the time to volunteer the way you want to, you can also support a group or organization financially.

Activation

How are you setting yourself up for success?

Answer the following questions:

- Does your job define you? Do you place your value in your job? If so, how much of your value is in your job?

- Are you holding back from asking a girl out because you don't feel proud of your job?

- What is the point of being discouraged because of your job? Where will that attitude take you? Or on the other end of the spectrum, have you become cocky because of your job or career?

- Do you understand that God loves you more than you judge yourself? Are you willing to be proud of who you are, looking beyond what your job may suggest about your value?

- How can you work for the Lord?

Include God as much as possible in your work, even if you're the guy in the back washing the dishes. Talk to Him while you are working and thank Him for His provision. Ask Him your questions about the future.

Single Life Tip

Stay busy, be yourself, and don't settle.

— Daron

4. Workin' It

5
I'd Like a Scoop of Hope[11]

I think the whole "trying to be authentic" fad is really healthy but not if it keeps you from believing that God is good or if it shuts down your faith and hope. Let me explain what I mean.

For a time, I chose to focus just on how I felt. I wanted to be "real," and I thought that was how you did it. I tried to be serious and somber toward my belief in God, but this meant I couldn't have any faith, because faith brings joy and I couldn't have any joy. If I were going to be excited, it needed to be for something unrelated to God, because anything else wouldn't be "real."

I have since determined this way of thinking is lame.

Steve Backlund says that trying to stay somber and serious in your walk with God is actually an attempt to be in control. Believing in God means you believe even in those aspects of Him that are not all that somber. You believe He is good, that He is love and life, that He is joy, holiness, power, and freedom. You believe He can do anything. Trying to be in control blocks your intimacy with Him and keeps you from really knowing who He is.

---

[11] This past spring, I lived it up at an Igniting Hope conference with Steve and Wendy Backlund. I strongly recommend reading and watching everything from this fun and encouraging couple. Much of this chapter was influenced by what I've learned from Igniting Hope Ministries, Steve's preaching, the Igniting Hope conference, and Wendy's book *Victorious Emotions*.

5. I'd Like a Scoop of Hope

Being authentic doesn't mean you have to focus solely on what your feelings are saying. It doesn't mean you have to let your emotions take you wherever they want to go and that somehow, by really feeling these things and getting in touch with them, you will become a whole person. Obviously, it is important to know how you feel, but it isn't healthy to let your feelings rule your life.[12]

There is a time to grieve, to feel pain deeply and not shut it down. But it is also good to move on. We don't have to succumb to despair, hopelessness, or other negative feelings and allow them to control how we behave.

But at the same time, the opposite of sobriety is not healthy or "real" either. Being happy all the time because you think you have to be or that it's a sign of a "real" Christian isn't authentic; it robs you of experiencing reality and actually dealing with the pain. Having joy doesn't mean you have to laugh or smile all the time; joy is a choice. You can laugh at hard circumstances, at yourself, at life, at mistakes, at funny things—and at lies, because you know the truth and the lie is stupid.

What Is Hope?

Like joy, hope doesn't discount our feelings or push them down underground. It doesn't mean just being positive or smiling a

---

[12] Wendy Backlund, *Victorious Emotions: Creating a Framework for a Happier You* (Redding, CA: Steve Backlund, 2017).

lot, nor does it mean ignoring pain or being lazy, waiting for something to happen.

Hope doesn't say, "If God would just provide a wife for me, I would really serve Him." Or "I just hope something good will happen, because then I will be content. Once I am content, then I will be thankful." No, hope is very similar to faith, and we have faith for things we do not see (Heb. 11:1). If we could see them, it wouldn't be faith. If I hope for sunshine and today is sunny, there is no need for me to have faith for a sunny day.

For a long time, my experiences in life seemed to suggest that it was getting more and more challenging to find someone compatible. Having hope in this area became hard for me. Why should I continue to hope when I was so easily disappointed? Wouldn't it be a lot less painful *not* to hope? I wanted to get married and repeatedly found myself growing frustrated as I considered my age and how I was still single.

At that point in my life, what should I have put my hope in? Should I have put my hope in my desire to get married one day? Well, that just led me to disappointment. I would get excited about a girl and build her up in my head until she seemed perfect for me, and then I would crash hard when it didn't work out.

Or should I have put my hope in my attraction to my future spouse? I found myself thinking that my wife had to be hot from the get-go, and the moment I saw her, I would know I wanted to marry her. It took me a while to realize that as long as my hope was in my future wife, I would be disappointed.

5. I'd Like a Scoop of Hope

My hope needed to be in something greater.

When I was thirty years old, I remember thinking how unfair it was that I was single. A lot of guys around me were pretty messed up, yet they had amazing girlfriends and were getting married. Then there was me. I was volunteering at church, working hard, staying in shape, paying off debt, and had really good community . . . but no girlfriend.

I found myself getting mad at God because I was still single and guys who had worse issues than I did were getting the girls. I got so fed up with it that I eventually grew tired of trying to be a good Christian. What good had it brought me? I thought, *I have never rebelled and I am sick of being good. I am sick of being afraid of losing God's love for me and feeling that I must be good in order for Him to love me. I am pissed off, so I'm going to do some bad things. I don't care about trying to be good anymore. What has it got me? I've wanted to get married so bad for so long and it hasn't happened. Why haven't You given me a wife? I am great with kids; I love women and I treat them well. I care about people.* Yet God still hadn't given me this thing I wanted the most.

So in my anger, I started going to strip clubs in Portland, getting lap dances, and drinking a bunch. I had to have the alcohol—I wouldn't have been able to stomach what I was doing without numbing my judgment.

My anger toward God lasted for three months before Eric, my pastor at the time, said something to me that rocked my world.

"It isn't God's fault," he said. "You're single because of your choices."

What? But slowly I realized he was right.

I had set marriage too high in my life, and at the same time, I'd subconsciously thought I didn't have it together enough to pursue a woman. I had debt. I was struggling with porn to the point I thought I didn't deserve to be married. I was dealing with it and not hiding it, but I was still struggling. So yes, I could see how it was my choice to be single. It hurt me to acknowledge this, but Eric's words were helpful.

Taking responsibility for yourself is a good thing. When you're trying to find a job, you don't turn down interviews because you aren't perfect or happen to lack in certain areas. You don't just sit around the house thinking about jobs and decide to skip out when an interview comes up. The same is true with dating. In my thirties I should have dated more. I should have accepted myself more, shown myself love, and not focused so much on my weaknesses.

In his recent book *God Is Good*, Bill Johnson discusses God's nature. No matter what my circumstances are, God is good. No matter how messed up this world is, no matter how rejected or how lonely and left behind I feel, God is still good.

It wasn't His fault that I was single. I made those decisions, using the free will He gave me.

5. I'd Like a Scoop of Hope

God Is So Good

What does believing in the goodness of God have to do with hope?

Believing that God is good is both a privilege and a comfort. Instead of putting our hope in getting married one day or in having our circumstances line up a certain way, it is much better to put our hope in the goodness of God. Everything else will let us down, but He never will. Not a single time.

I can say with full confidence that I do not have everything I want in life. Should I blame God for that? What possible good would come from blaming God, who is holy, for something I think is bad? He is just, He is kind, He is wisdom, He is love, He is life. He doesn't merely possess these things; He is these things. It doesn't help me to think that the Holy One has given me something bad.

Yes, it can be difficult, even painful, to be single sometimes, especially on Thanksgiving, Christmas, Easter, your birthday, or when your whole family gets together. The sadness can creep in on these holidays every year, but does that pain mean that God is mean, doesn't care, or has forgotten you? No, it doesn't.

In the gloom of the day, after yet another date didn't work out, it can be challenging to believe the truth that we haven't been left behind. We have to deal with all the questions that arise: Will I ever get married? What's wrong with me? Does God even like me? Am I somehow on the "not included" list?

Again, it is okay to grieve for a season. It's okay to be sad. Even though I was repeating amazing declarations of God's truth every day, I still found myself feeling sad and lonely. But I began to realize I didn't have to have it all together because God *does* have it all together.

When I really thought about it, I knew that God has always been good. So the best gift I could give myself was to hope in a good God.

The "facts" may say that I am failing at something or someone rejected me, but the truth—that I am loved perfectly and there is no condemnation for those in Christ Jesus—is a bigger and more powerful fact (Rom. 8:1). I am not denying the reality of the situation. Instead, I am believing in a greater reality in the midst of my earthly reality. Personally, I think it takes more energy *not* to hope in a good God and to be depressed and angry, thinking He doesn't give a rip about me.

Making a good decision about something I'm hoping for isn't easy when I don't like myself. In that position, thinking those thoughts, it's difficult to be strong or powerful. If I believe that God is good, that means I have to prepare myself for good things to happen, which takes responsibility. I have a part to play in positioning myself for good things to happen and to see God as good regardless of my circumstances.

If I think God isn't good, then I am not required to hope and there is nothing for me to be responsible for. I no longer need to prepare for His goodness, provision, faithfulness, creativity, life, and so forth. I can be passive, just a blob on the couch, because there is nothing for me to hope in.

My point is, we all need to receive as much goodness from God as possible. "Preparing" for His goodness doesn't mean we have to try to be perfect; that is the power of God working within us because of Jesus. As we surrender to His righteousness (Rom. 3:21–22), we are viewed as spotless and blameless because of Him. We cannot add to the work on the cross. Putting all the burden on our own shoulders and trying to be a good Christian gets old after a while, and we start to think that sin is more exciting. Being a good Christian is something that happens naturally when we abide in Christ. Our hearts change and our behavior follows suit.

You get to receive as much goodness from God as possible. All you have to do is believe the truth of who you are as a son of the King (Eph. 5:1). All the resources God has are at your disposal. All the comfort in the world, all the power in the world, and all the love in the world is available for you. God is in you. He is not just present with you, but He is actually *inside* you.[13] You don't have to depend on yourself for this kind of hope to exist.

It takes more energy to reject God's perfect love for you than it does to surrender to it and believe it. That is the first step:

---

[13] I encourage you to listen to the song "Take Courage" by Kristene DiMarco (Bethel Music).

surrendering your preconceived ideas about God and just believing His love for you.

For me, having hope means receiving love. I know very well what it is like not to love myself. For years, I punished myself because of some sick pressure to perform, because I wanted to be someone different—the kind of man who would be a better match for a certain woman or who would be liked by someone I wanted to like me. But every time I give up the idea of being the judge and instead hold on to my dreams and trust that God is good, I can settle down and enjoy myself, which allows me to be a man who is a giver, not a taker.

When I hope in God's goodness, I understand that my circumstances do not define me. They do not change who I am. Whether I have $16.94 or $1,694 in the bank, I am the same person—I am my Dad's beloved son. I am in His family and a citizen of heaven (Eph. 2:19).

And *that* hope does not disappoint. Why? Because it always exists. It is always here, and it won't slide through my fingers because it doesn't depend on anything in my life—it is dependent on God. And I get to depend on Him, for He is good.

When I am filled with hope like this, I can be a man. With hope I can be unselfish and scale any wall, as King David wrote in Psalm 18. With hope I can move forward in relationships, work, and other situations in my life and not stay trapped in self-pity. With hope I can take risks.

As you can see, hope is a powerful thing.

5. I'd Like a Scoop of Hope

Analyzing, Awkwardness, and Assumptions

A few years ago, I was interested in more than one woman at the same time. I had plenty of options for where I put my hope while I thought about what to say, what to invite this one or that one to, the timing involved, how to be friends first, what my actions were communicating, how to be a man and a gentleman, and on it went. I found myself analyzing everything and hoping I wouldn't stumble into an awkward situation.

As we think about awkward moments and how we sure don't want anything to be awkward again, fear can start to creep in. We can begin to worry about what a woman thinks and then worry about being too forward or too bold. What if we express our interest only to find out that it's completely one sided? What if this messes up our friendship? What if we're not "good enough" for this particular woman or what if we don't click?

We could analyze the relationship right out the door before giving it a chance, but what good would that do?

Some of us may argue, "Analyzing a relationship ahead of time will protect me from getting hurt."

Yes, perhaps more carefully analyzing a past relationship would have protected me from pain, but analyzing doesn't help when it comes from a critical or selfish mindset or is based in fear.

I found I was able to pursue a lady more easily when I placed my hope in my Abba Father, who loves me perfectly and is with me. My peace was greater when I knew that my heart's desires were good. It was always better when I didn't worry about my friend's potential rejection or that asking her out would ruin our friendship or make things awkward for our group of friends. That was one of the main things I used to worry about while dating: *How will this affect our circle of friends?* If she wasn't interested in me, I would feel humiliated.

Would you prefer to spend your time analyzing a relationship or pursuing one? Do you want to focus on avoiding awkwardness, or would it be easier just to be honest about how you feel and enjoy being yourself, not worrying about rejection to the point of being uptight? Is it actually helpful to assume your pursuit of a girl will hurt your friendship or cause tension in your circle of friends? Or is it better to express your true self and your interest in her, trusting that you will still be good friends regardless of the outcome? As Wayne Gretzky and Michael Jordan have said, "You miss 100 percent of the shots you don't take."

Expectations: Bigger Than a Four-letter Word

Humans were made to worship something, and when we worship our Creator, it makes us whole. Because we walk according to the "grain" within us, we find reward and peace in worshiping God.

When we place our hope in a good God, we worship Him with faith. If we sing His praises but all the while think He isn't good, we won't be worshiping Him accurately because He really is good.

5. I'd Like a Scoop of Hope

I find enormous freedom when I worship with faith. In these moments, I am not worshiping to get something from Him, viewing Him as some kind of genie or a divine slot machine. He is not a calculator with set formulas already programmed in. But I am worshiping in agreement with who He is. When I agree with Him, I can see what He is doing. I can see more how *He* sees, which makes it easier to have hope and not be depressed, because I am seeing myself, my life, and my future with expectancy.

Practically speaking, expectancy means believing good without limits. Because God is good, I am expectant that I will see breakthrough beyond my imagination.

Expectancy and *expectation* are two different words. Expectancy goes beyond expectation because my belief is in God, who cannot be limited. Expectations, meanwhile, are what I can see happening. They form my ideas or a list of things I want, what I expect to happen, or what I don't expect to happen. They're more about what's in it for me. There is a limit to expectations, and as a human, I tend to base my joy on whether or not my expectations are met. I can actually predict ahead of time that if something does not happen, I will be let down. What if a woman I'm getting to know doesn't meet my expectations or treat me the way I think I deserve? I could pull back or end the budding relationship simply because I wanted a specific thing to happen and my expectations weren't met.

But with expectancy, it is totally a different ballgame. I know she is who she is, and even after taking her out, buying her dinner, and giving her gifts, I don't have to expect her to do something in return. Instead, I am confident that she is still the great person I know and that her heart is toward me. My hope is in something above human limitations.

When I expect God to be good, I am not depressed when I look around and don't see anyone I am interested in. It doesn't discourage me. I don't even wonder, "Am I interested in her? Or what about that woman over there? Do I think she's attractive?" It just naturally happens that I see someone I know and I go up and talk to her. I don't even need to analyze if I "want" to talk to her or not. I just go and talk to her. I may be a little nervous about it, but I am going up to her out of the joy inside me, out of the understanding that God is good and He knows how to give me good gifts and I'm partnering with Him. I am "opening the gifts," you could say.

Expectancy in a good God fuels me to move forward with joy and boldness. Expectations that put pressure on me, or on a woman I may or may not be interested in, build walls that block the flow.

A lot of people say it's good not to have any expectations when you're just getting to know someone. Yes, that mindset can remove pressure, but it also can lead a man to be passive. I find that trying not to have expectations invites men to sit back and relax instead of going after someone and taking risks. With expectancy, we look for our needs to be met by God and not by people. But if our goal is to avoid expectations, it subtly pulls at our desire for relationship.

5. I'd Like a Scoop of Hope

With expectancy, not only do other people look different, but I look different as well. This freedom allows me to be loving toward others because my needs are met by my perfect Dad, and I don't feel pressure to find that flawless woman who will meet my needs for me. This causes me to become more attractive because I am free to be who I am and feel no pressure to be perfect. It's hard to be attracted to someone who is trying to be perfect, because in the back of your mind, you kind of know those people will eventually find fault with you.

Activation

Where are you placing your hope?

Read Romans 8:38–39 and ask God to reveal to you how He sees you. My friend, you are so much more loved than you love yourself.

How do you see God? Ask Him to show you His goodness. I encourage you to record in a journal any areas of this chapter that brought up questions inside you as well as those areas you feel like you should ponder more deeply. Where can you apply expectancy in your relationships and other areas of your life?

Single Life Tip

Love yourself and create a complete life that thrills you. You and your potential mate are two whole people coming together to have and create a solid relationship. You don't want two broken people coming together hoping that the relationship will fix and fulfill you. A relationship is hard enough without that pressure. And lastly, sleep in. Enjoy nights of uninterrupted sleep. And naps.

— Ashly

5. I'd Like a Scoop of Hope

6

Worshiping God by How You Treat Your Date

I recently took my friend Michael out to dinner to celebrate a really good date he'd gone on. This particular young lady was the most beautiful woman he had seen up to that point, and they had many important things in common, including a passion for dancing and acting. The two or three hours he'd spent with her earlier that day had blown by like a jet in the sky.

So we went to Final Draft Brewery downtown. While he ordered dinner, I had a fine beer and decided on a lava chocolate cake with ice cream for dessert.

I wanted to hear all about what happened with this girl. And more importantly, I wanted to encourage him and share some perspective on dating. I was really impressed with how Michael was handling the situation. He had an excellent, Jesus-like approach toward this woman that looked like wanting the best for her, being a good listener, and asking her riveting questions.

The way you treat a woman is worship unto God. As a man, you are representing Jesus to her. As you get to know a woman, it is best—and brings the man out of you—to be focused on giving to her, not on what she can give to you. Jesus represents unselfishness, and that is how you were made and even designed. Even the physical act of lovemaking represents how a man takes the initiative and gives to a woman.

6. Worshiping God by How You Treat Your Date

Biblically speaking, when you live in an understanding way with your wife, your prayers will not be hindered (1 Pet. 3:7). Honoring your wife is, therefore, one of the most important things you can do in life. As a single man, you get to practice honoring your wife right now, even if you haven't met her yet. Have you ever heard the phrase "Practice like you play"? It means that if you want to play the big game really well, then you'd better practice really well—as if you were playing the big game. That is even truer in life than it is on the ball field.

So according to Scripture, God honors your prayers when you are understanding toward your wife. This means, first, that it is possible to live in an understanding way with her. And second, it is also possible to be sensitive, to listen, and to honor her. You are a smart man when you honor women.

All these elements—listening, initiating, taking risks, and providing for a woman—are worship. Why? Because whatever you do, you get to do it unto the glory of God (1 Cor. 10:31). Right now, because you and your future wife are still single, she is God's. She doesn't belong to you. Not until you are married does she belong to you, and at that point, you belong to her as well.

Marriage is a good idea for several reasons. It makes us more Christlike and brings God glory. It reveals more of His nature to us and, of course, helps us be fruitful and multiply by having children. God says it is not good for man to be alone. If the point of marriage is about giving to others, growing in Christ, and learning how to be more Christlike, then the dating scene is at its best when it follows the same goals. Obviously, I am not saying that you can't be Christlike without a woman in your life. But why would you carry a dating perspective that is contrary to what you want your marriage to be like?

As men, we get to lay our lives down for our wives as Christ did for the church, for all of us. That is what you get to do for your date. This looks different for some, but practically speaking, here is what laying your life down for your date can mean.

You get to initiate interest in her and take that first risk of rejection. This represents your giving to her. You can ask her out in a way that is both non-manipulative and bold; it isn't needy or pushy. Tell her you are interested in her simply because you are, not to get something from her. Get to know each other, to have fun, to share interests. This, of course, will look a little different if you're approaching a woman you've known for a while, someone who is your friend.

You get to treat this woman *very* well. She is the climax of God's creation. She is beautiful and has a heart you need to value, honor, treasure, and protect. All that is true in Scripture about love you get to represent to her.

Treating her well looks like being respectful to her, opening the doors for her, paying for part or all of every excursion with her, asking her questions, and letting her talk most of the time. Be honest. Be yourself. When you are transparent, you are giving an accurate account of who you are. It means you are more interested in honoring God than even in impressing your date.

6. Worshiping God by How You Treat Your Date

Worshiping God with your date means you have given this woman over to the Lord. Either out loud or in your heart, you have prayed something like this:

> *God, I want to honor You and this woman during our time together. I want and declare that You are the center of my life, You are the One who gives me good gifts, and You know what You are doing. She is Yours, and I will treat her as if she will be another man's wife someday. I will treat her as Your daughter and represent You because I am Your son. She is my sister and I am her brother.*

Flirting

In 2003, I met a woman I had a lot of fun with. She loved my sense of humor, and I could make her laugh so easily. She was funny too, and I flirted with her big time. However, I knew I wasn't interested in her romantically.

I know all about flirting—believe me! There is nothing wrong with flirting in itself. But I will say that if you notice you're starting to feel prideful because of all the attention you're getting from this girl, beware! Yes, it feels super, super good to have all of this interest from her, and there is nothing wrong with that. But being a real man will take you much further than gloating or a self-promoting mindset will. Just check yourself or allow others to check you for you. At the end of the day, I hurt this woman's feelings because I showed interest in her that I didn't actually mean.

Flirting from the wrong motivation is the opposite of being a man and the opposite of love. Don't make your date about you. Don't fall into the trap of thinking you're a better man because she is with you. You get your value from being a child of God, from being perfectly loved by Him. If your hope is in the woman you're with, eventually you'll find yourself disappointed.

Don't strive after this girl or that girl, because that won't be good for you in the long run. Be a giver, not a taker. Be humble, be gentle, be real, and represent yourself accurately. Have things to share with her about yourself that will invite her into your world. In addition to listening well and focusing on her, open up about yourself and share about the things you have done, your goals, mistakes, failures, and what you've learned.

If this date is worship, it means that no matter how things go on the date, you're going to be okay. It means that her interests are worth listening to. The words you speak to her are filtered through your desire to protect her heart and treat her in the same way you would treat Jesus. Treat her like the princess she is.

As far as having fun during your date, that represents Jesus too. This is called freedom, which develops more and more as you grow comfortable with each other. Freedom is another reason it's easier to pursue a girl who is already your friend.

But either way you slice it, have fun. Be led with truth instead of the fear of making a mistake.

6. Worshiping God by How You Treat Your Date

Put God at the Center of Your Date

In your daily life, you commit things to God. You live with wisdom at your job, with your friends, and as you follow your pursuits. Just as you love to be free from fear and what other people are thinking, you can have a date that is free from fear and filled with freedom and joy.

How do you do this? You walk in love, believing you are loved and that your value is not based on how well the date goes. You are free to be yourself because this is who you are and you are representing yourself to her. You are more focused on the good things God is doing in your life and on what the woman is involved in than you are in trying to impress her. You aren't afraid of failure, which means you can relax—and relaxing allows you to be goofy and coherent, have quality things to say, be creative, and actually laugh, have fun, and be lighthearted. That, my man, is how you introduce freedom and joy to your soul.

Another important ingredient is having a thankful heart during everyday activities. If you can do this, your thankfulness and gratitude for life will just ooze from you during your date. Who you are when you are alone is the biggest indicator of who you are in general. As you have quality days, your dates will reflect this and also be quality.

Stay Focused, My Friend

As you spend time with and listen to this other person, learn to see the gold in her—that which is her best. See Jesus in her, and bring enthusiasm and hope for her dreams and passions. Encourage her. Listen with your ears and with your heart. Actually look into her eyes when you are listening, not around at other people and what they are doing. Don't look at the TV up in the corner but remember your goal for the date—it's to connect with her, not to catch glimpses of the ballgame.

Be thankful for your date even before it starts, and be thankful during and after it as well. Thank God for who you are, for the possible awkward parts of your time (which will help prevent any), for the good times, for who this woman is, and for this opportunity. Thank God for making such an amazing woman. Thank God for who He is in your life and for providing for all your needs. Thank Him for the joy He's given you, for making you into a man, for how you are made.

If the date ends up not going well, if you were super nervous or awkward, or if she didn't show much interest, don't hate yourself. It's okay. Even with dating, there is no condemnation for you because you are in Christ Jesus (Rom. 8:1). Thank God for loving you no matter what. The more you are thankful, the more you will walk in His will, for His will for you is to give thanks in all things (1 Thess. 5:16–18). You will be amazed at how differently you begin to view yourself, other people, and your life when you look around through a thankful lens.

6. Worshiping God by How You Treat Your Date

Remember that no one *has* to like you. This woman is free not to connect with you, and you are free to be nervous. It isn't the end of the world. It may not be pleasant, but it doesn't have to be terrible. In the end, what she thinks of you does not determine who you are.

Forgive yourself as Christ has forgiven you. If you realize you're at a point of self-loathing because of something you said or did and now you feel foolish, repent of your judgment toward yourself as well as prideful thinking. That's really what self-loathing is; it's thinking that you determine your value and that you need everything to work out the way you want it to in order to be happy. Yes, it can be miserable when dates don't go well, but not liking yourself or punishing yourself in some way in hopes of doing better next time doesn't work. Period. I've tried it and I know what it's like. So don't put that kind of pressure on yourself.

Activation

You are God's son. Your life is His. Do your best and, when necessary, mourn your painful date. But then move on.

Worship is connection with God. I pray you have increased connection with Him as well as increased expressions of worship that happen more and more outside of church. I pray you're able to see what you do as worship unto God. Whether at work, on a date, being a good friend, being a man and taking responsibility, serving others, being truthful and authentic, being bold about your weaknesses, or whatever else you are doing—it can all be done unto the glory of God. He is with you and He delights in you (Rom. 5:1–2, 12:1, 14:8).

Write down how you can include God in your everyday activities by thanking Him, committing things to Him, and listening to what He has to say. What Scriptures come to mind?

How can you, personally, include God and be mindful of Him while you are socializing or going on a date? Talk to a friend about this if you feel you need feedback.

Single Life Tip

Live without fear. Reject it at every turn, single or not, and your life will be an extraordinary expression of God's image in you.

— Espirito

6. Worshiping God by How You Treat Your Date

7

How to Be Fully Present and Build Community

I moved to Redding, California, to be with my family, who have been in the process of trickling down to California for the last eight years or so. Moving from Oregon, my home state, to Redding brought some cultural changes, as you may imagine. Also I took a pay cut for my new job and was paying capital gains tax from selling my business in 2014, so I needed a low-rent place. I decided to live in a house filled with students and former students because I wanted to get into the culture of the Bethel School of Supernatural Ministry without actually attending the school. That meant sharing a bedroom with someone else.

I was forty-two years old at the time and hadn't shared a bedroom since I was nineteen. So this was a sacrifice for me that, thankfully, didn't last too long. I received a nice raise at work and was able to move into my own room.

I wanted to be close to family and get involved at Bethel Church, so I was willing to make these sacrifices.

And I'll be honest. I thought it likely that in a church the size of Bethel, there would be a higher chance of my meeting the woman of my dreams.

It's been a blast being around my nephew and niece, my brother and his wife, and my parents. We've gone hiking, hunting, camping, and swimming and had lots of Sunday lunches together. In addition to my family, I had built-in, constant community because I'd chosen to live with students. Being the youngest in my family, it has always been easier for me to hang out with peers or older friends, but in Redding I've been able to grow in my comfort level with younger people. So this has been good for me.

Being known is the rock star of thriving. To conquer the world, each of us needs a band of brothers. You can try to be a lone ranger, but it just won't be as fun, or as healthy. You can also have only guy friends, but how will this help you learn to be comfortable with women? With a group of friends come all the fun times, the giving-each-other-a-hard-time times, being there for each other, praying for one another, going on crazy adventures, celebrating each other's birthdays, having game nights and worship nights, and making awesome memories that will be with you forever. All these things are good.

Having close friends is rewarding and helpful. Even if you have only one close friend to share with, one person to walk through life with you, this can help you through every bump or mountain you face.

Part of being a close friend is sharing the difficult or vulnerable areas of your life. When I am telling my buddy about my weaknesses, or how I really feel, I can be fully present with him. Being fully present allows me to build a foundation with this other man, which gives me the stability I need so I can share my pain, victories, and goals with him, instead of isolating and numbing myself.

What do you do when you isolate? Maybe you don't call it that; many people call it escaping. What do you do to forget about your day at work or about the pain of your relationship with your parents? Maybe you're still trying to get over that rejection from the last girl you went out with or perhaps didn't go out with.

Do you watch TV the whole evening? Look at porn? Do you eat everything in sight? Do you read fantasies all night? Play video games? Watch sports or the news for hours? Are you on social media all evening? Some of these things are not bad in themselves, but they become unhealthy when they take all or most of our time. We need interaction with real live human beings. This means actually talking to someone else in person or on the phone. Not just texting.

Imagine yourself several years down the road. What do you hope to have accomplished by then? Do you want your biggest accomplishment to be that you accumulated countless hours of mind-numbing activities? Even right now, if your pain is greater than your desire for a better life, or you couldn't care less about anything but feeling numb on the inside, I will tell you there is an easier way.

If you desire to have healthy friendships, to receive love, to love yourself, to love others, and to love that girl you're interested in, choose what you say yes to. The easier way is to tell someone what you are going through, get prayed for, get a hug, get encouraged, and know you are not alone. The emotional pain you are going through is not bigger than God. There is a solution.

7. How to Be Fully Present and Build Community

It is much harder to hold all that pain inside and let the pressure build. Holding on to your bitterness is like taking poison, and it will end up killing you. It's harder to be bitter than to let go. Try it and you'll see. It takes more energy to be bitter, and eventually a bitter person will crash and burn.

Telling others what you're going through allows you to heal. Holding things inside or isolating from others causes you to reject truth and the very light that could set you free. But telling others takes the darkness and peels it open so light can replace it, and the journey toward peace and freedom begins.

This is why having a circle of friends is essential for a healthy life. We were built for friendships, not simply to be spectators or to be entertained. I am so thankful for the amazing friends I've had over the years. From backpacking on Mt. Hood to the hilarious times at restaurants, from hiking, praying for each other, and going to home groups to having game nights and helping each other move—whatever it was, it was with great people.

Don't sit at home hoping that someone will text and invite you to go do something. Go be a friend. Purposefully make memories, and choose to be fully present with the people around you.

Go After Community

Part of being a man and pursuing a woman is being intentional and initiating relationships and community. You do this by being active and creating something, not just letting everyone else do it for you.

Back in 1986, my family was living in a house with no heat. We had just moved back to Gresham after being in Colorado for a year, and we didn't have much. But our home group did. That year at Christmas, we had the most presents we'd ever had. Our group took amazing care of us, and to this day, we still treasure those friendships. That is the power of building community with others—you don't have to do anything alone.

Before I moved to Redding, I lived in a house in Salem that was managed by an amazing guy named Kevin Franklin. He and his best friend, Austin, started a worship night that took place every other Sunday evening, and they called it The Refreshing. To this day, it still brings fifty to eighty young people from all over Salem and surrounding areas for hours of worship and prophetic words as well as a powerful communion time. These nights typically go until about 12:30 in the morning.

After moving to Redding, I missed those worship nights, so I started hosting worship nights once a month at my house. My housemates and I invited our friends, and my housemate Justin led worship. I just facilitated, sharing a few verses and trying to be led by the Holy Spirit. This is one way I purposefully built community for myself, because I knew how much I needed it.

Another great way I have connected with others is through BNI or Business Network International. One of the most successful business-networking groups in the world, it has helped me feel more connected to Redding and with other professionals in the area, and I have grown in my leadership skills. Every week, we each give a forty-second presentation about our business and mention what our "ask" is for that week. An "ask" is the specific business referral we would like that week. The group is effective and fun, and it's become like family for me.

If you're a business owner, manager, or have a marketing position, I highly recommend joining or starting a BNI group. Rotary, Chamber, and other service organizations are also excellent leadership and growth opportunities that give back to their communities.

Going to such a large church, it is easy just to say hi to the people I recognize and not really get to know anyone at a deeper level. But true "church" happens in small groups. Instead of looking at how many people you don't know at your church, it's best to focus on a small group. Be thankful for who you do know because this will open your heart to meeting new people more easily when the opportunity arises. No one wants to hang out with someone who complains all the time that other people aren't reaching out to them. So be a man and introduce yourself to someone. Get involved. Home groups, classes, and volunteer opportunities are good ways to get plugged into a larger community.

One group I attend is a men's group called Man Alive. In addition to purity, the group focuses on facing our pain and challenges, living in reality, being a man, leading, being healthy, pursuing our dreams, having community and that band of brothers, and how to pursue women. I am willing to go to this group because I want other guys to speak into my life. I also want encouragement and to be the best man I can be.[14]

My friend Britt and I also led a Single Life Workshop e-course life group from Nothing Hidden Ministries.[15]

My point is, I have seen the benefit of being intentional. Therefore, I purposefully choose to grow in being authentically known, facing my issues, making time for friends and family, and having fun while also pursuing my goals. Being intentional means you have a goal and you do it; you don't just passively let everyone else do things for you. You make plans, you invite a friend, and then you go and do it.

If there isn't a group you can join at your church, start something. And if that doesn't work, try starting an unofficial group with your friends. Be consistent and meet often, so you can build your tribe.

There are ways to make the most of the opportunities you're given. I've been involved in some amazing singles' and college-age groups. If you don't have such groups at your church, start meeting with friends on a regular basis. Start a home group. Have worship nights, game nights, and parties—do life together.

If you would like to be involved in a group, be a man and make it happen. Don't just rely on the ladies to organize everything.

---

[14] You can watch or listen to this group at www.imanalive.com.
[15] It costs less than $100 to purchase the e-course, and you can go through it at your own pace. You can also invite friends over and take the course together.

7. How to Be Fully Present and Build Community

Just because they may be better at it than you doesn't mean you get to be passive and let them initiate all the social events. I'm not trying to tell you what to do; I'm just letting you know that if you take a risk and step out, you will have a rewarding experience.

Be known. Make friends outside of church. Coworkers, neighbors, people at the gym—you get the idea.

And whatever you do, be thankful for the people in your life. Thankfulness breathes creativity and ideas, and it allows you to see opportunities that you wouldn't see if you were stuck complaining about your lack of opportunity.

Who are your people? Write down a list of people you want to invest in and focus on them, keeping in mind that it isn't good to be so spread out that you can't go deep with anyone.

All of us need close friendships in our lives for the same reason a tree needs thick roots that grow deep into the earth: Our "roots" hold us up so we can grow, take the winds as they come, and not topple. These friends who go deep with us help us mature and become people others can look up to. They help provide shade, beauty, and comfort for us, which in turn allows us to be equipped to help others.

Community is a beautiful way to meet and get to know an amazing woman. It offers a secure foundation for one member of that community to become much more important to you over time. Because I had strong community and good friends, one of my female friends, Melissa, had an easier time getting to know me better. She was able to see me being real and how I interacted with other people. My community and close friends gave her the opportunity to find out if I was the same person in different settings when it wasn't just the two of us alone.

This turned out really well for me.

But I'll tell you more about that later.

Activation

Write down the rewards of isolation versus the rewards of being in community.

List several friends, family, and coworkers you would like to do something with, and then find an event or create one around an interest all of you share. Contact those people and invite them to join you. Invite them at least a week in advance so there is more of a chance they will show up, and request that they RSVP.

Ask God for community and about the people He wants to be in your life.

Single Life Tip

Laugh a lot. Serve wherever you can. Leverage your strength and energy in the places that matter most to you. Climb things. Change something other people say cannot be changed. Befriend small children and elderly folks and people you look up to and people who are wildly different than you and people who seem like they don't have a lot to give.

— Christina

7. How to Be Fully Present and Build Community

8
Hi! My Name Is _____ and I'm Lonely

Have you ever shopped for a date online?

For a few years, I had accounts with about seven different dating sites. It was sometimes a lot of fun and other times discouraging. Occasionally I had interest from girls I didn't want to be interested in me, and most of the time, it seemed like the girls I was interested in ignored me.

As I scanned countless profile pictures, I found myself on an emotional rollercoaster that I couldn't endure long term. I soon grew numb to the highs and lows, and looking for a date online became almost like a part-time evening job. Would someone I was interested in reply to me?

The more I worked at it, the more disappointed I felt. Obviously, many guys have met their wives from online dating, and there are thousands of amazing people who are using it. I don't mean to rag on it. I had quite a few dates from online dating sites, but overall, online dating just seemed to feed my loneliness.

I am someone who can feel lonely quite easily. If I don't have plans for the weekend or if I'm bored, I can start feeling lonely. Even though I have lots of friends and family—people I could easily call or connect with—there are times I still feel lonely.

8. Hi! My Name Is____and I'm Lonely

Have you ever felt like you were alone even though you had plenty of people around you? Have you ever been an active member of a weekly small group and still felt lonely? What's up with that?

It is possible for me to be open and vulnerable with a friend, allowing this person to see me completely as I am, and still feel lonely. Have you experienced that strange phenomenon? It seems there is more to feeling connected than hanging out with friends, or even being vulnerable with them.

What should a man do to keep from feeling lonely? I've met people who have only a few friends, yet they aren't lonely the way I can be sometimes. Then there are those people who have *lots* of friends and still feel lonely.

I can also feel lonely because my group of friends has shifted and I don't have the same friends I used to. This can quickly become an issue in my thinking because if I compare one set of friends with another set of friends, one set will never quite measure up. It's easy to be critical this way and keep people at a distance.

Loneliness can masquerade as disappointment because I don't have something I desperately want. In this case, loneliness is much like emptiness.

For years, I often felt lonely when I was at my folks' house on a Sunday afternoon surrounded by family. I felt that way because I was the only single person there, the only one without a family of his own. My brother had his wife and two kids. My parents had each other, plus all of us. And then there was me. Single Uncle Judd.

But this is what we need to remember about loneliness. When we are carrying the expectation that we should be married, then wherever we are or whatever we are doing, we will feel lonely. When we are focusing on what we *lack*, it is very easy for us to have lonely feelings.

If we start criticizing everything about ourselves or about our lives, nothing will measure up and everyone will let us down, even ourselves.

The answer is to surrender to the goodness of God. This will help remove the anxiety and pressure, and it will lead to rest and peace. The lonely feelings will drift away.

Whenever we believe we are lacking, we will feel lonely no matter what we have or who we are with. We will feel like victims.

What actively works to keep us from feeling lonely? Believing the truth that we have plenty. We are citizens of God's kingdom. He is our Provider, and we have every spiritual blessing (Ps. 16:5–8; Gal. 4:6; Eph. 1:3, 2:19; 1 Pet. 2:9). It may be that right now we don't have something we want, but the truth is, God is good and we are loved perfectly.

That, my friend, is powerful. It is a truth that can be used in any area of life, for anyone in any stage.

I remember a family dinner a few years ago when I purposefully chose not to focus on the fact that I was single. As a result, something really amazing happened. I had a great time joking around, being silly, and showing affection. I was at peace because I was living in love and not in fear.

Making the decision to look through the lenses of love is incredibly empowering. When we choose to be powerful, we find freedom, which brings joy and fulfillment and allows us to expand God's kingdom, do His good will, and bless others by giving selflessly. The benefits of being a powerful person could fill entire books by themselves.

When I feel like I am depending on others for my satisfaction, I am playing the role of a victim and it is super easy for me to be disappointed.

When I believe the lie that a certain person needs to say hi to me, or that I need to be friends with this other person in order to feel good about myself, I have to be careful because I am on the tracks of turmoil. And no healthy woman wants to hitch a ride with a guy who is in turmoil. Why would she? I would be asking her to accommodate my demanding self.

We *smell* when we are codependent. Other people can catch a whiff of us coming when we are desperate for affection and *need* them to like us.

Only by God's grace and knowing His love for us can we become powerful people who enjoy who we are without the approval of others. Bill Johnson, a pastor at Bethel

Church, says that grace enables us to obey God, to agree with Him. The law limits us, but grace enables.

When a man is healthy and walking in love, he's okay if he doesn't get to go over and talk to the woman he admires. He's okay if she's distracted or gives no visual signal about where they stand. He isn't passive; instead, he is confident that he has what he needs, that he can talk to her if he wants to, and he's fine if a conversation doesn't happen. He has let go of trying to control her. And this means freedom.

Activation

> Be thankful in all circumstances, for this is God's will for you who belong to Christ Jesus.
>
> 1 Thessalonians 5:18

Being thankful is the opposite of focusing on lack. If feeling lack leads to loneliness and unmet expectations, then being thankful leads to connection with God, ourselves, and other people. It allows us to see and believe how good God is, the spiritual abundance we have in Him, and all the physical and relational things He has already given us.

> But that's not all! Even in times of trouble we have a joyful confidence, knowing that our pressures will develop in us patient endurance. And patient endurance will refine our character, and proven character leads us back to hope.

And this hope is not a disappointing fantasy,
because we can now experience the endless
love of God cascading into our hearts through
the Holy Spirit who lives in us!

Romans 5:3–5 (TPT)

What are you thankful for? Specifically, what *challenges* are you thankful for?

Single Life Tip

Don't work at finding the woman you want . . . work at becoming the man God made you to be. That way, when you do find her, you're more of who God designed her to be with.

— Jennifer

9
Friendship and Striving

Gladiator is one of my all-time favorite films. I love it when Maximus goes before his men, looking them in the eyes before the upcoming battle, meeting them at their level, respecting them for being honorable—for sacrificing, being loyal, giving their all for Rome. When he steps onto the field, he greets each one and says, "Strength and honor." I love that scene.

We talked about honor in an earlier chapter, but here I want to make it a little more personal. Honor is a key heart condition for all relationships, including your relationship with yourself. As a man, don't try to be someone you are not. Honor yourself by being real. God didn't make a mistake when He made you, so there's no need to try to be someone else or even to try to be more of something.

Do you ever catch yourself thinking this way? *I have to be more _____ to meet a girl.* As Steve Backlund would say, let's laugh at that lie! The truth is, you are fine the way you are. Perhaps your character needs to grow in certain areas or you aren't as mature today as you will be next year, but you as a person don't need to be someone else.

Expressing Honor Toward a Woman

You can express honor toward a woman by listening. When you're out on a date, don't talk about yourself the whole time. Ask her questions you care about and show interest in what she is interested in; watch to see her come alive. It doesn't matter if you aren't interested in the same things. Just as you would do this with a male friend, spending time with him and getting to know him, do it here with her.

Focus on being her friend, remembering that being her friend is an opportunity and privilege. In a friendship, there are no demands, no need to manipulate, no need to control. There is only enjoying who you are and who she is, the passions the two of you have in life, your interests and dreams. As time goes on, you'll likely find that both of you are opening up more and more.

Being a friend also means that you are okay if things go the way you want them to and you're okay if they don't. To truly honor someone, you keep her best interest in mind; it's more than trying to get her to like you.

With men and women both, I struggle with trying to get others to like me. And that is not being powerful. I'm not trying to hold up power for power's sake, nor do I mean trying to get my own way so I can enjoy being a "powerful person." Being a powerful person allows me to love myself and love others because I am loved perfectly.

No one and nothing will change you. You get to change yourself. Getting married will not change how you relate to others, nor will it make your new wife respond the way you want her to. Marriage actually *highlights* who you are right now.

Striving

Anytime we start thinking that we are lacking and don't trust that God is good, it opens the door to striving, manipulation, and lust. A man doesn't need to lust after a woman's beautiful body or face when he is powerful, trusts God, and believes that he has everything he needs. He can see the same beautiful woman and appreciate her beauty but not look at her selfishly.

The devil wants to steal, kill, and destroy, but God the Father wants to fulfill (John 10:10). He wants us to live life to the fullest and for us to have joy and love and not be limited by fear (Rom. 8:15–16). If the devil can do so, he will try to convince us that we are not man enough or good enough to be in a relationship with a beautiful woman. If we believe this lie, it will keep us from talking to beautiful women and, instead, we will lust after them.

Our desires tell us about what we need. So if we find ourselves lusting after a woman, it means we need something, and we need to pay attention to that need. Perhaps you need adventure or physical activity or to take a risk; maybe you need comfort. Get these things met in a healthy way. Instead of just trying not to lust, take that desire and turn it into something according to how you are wired. Do something that makes you come alive like a hobby or social activity. Focusing on Jesus is always a good plan. Purity is a fruit or a result of being healthy, not the main goal.

Tell God how you feel and tell your friends as well. Use your frustration and funnel it toward something else: Work out, do something creative, worship, call a friend—but don't just numb the desire or medicate the frustration.

Thankfulness Will Break Lust

The beautiful women we see around us are real human beings just like we are. They are God's creation—our sisters. As single men, it is good to understand that what they have is theirs, not ours. This understanding is a gift. Having the right belief obliterates the battle of lust and loneliness. If I am trying *not* to notice a woman's body so I don't lust, I will fail and end up feeling miserable, weak, powerless, and not effective as a man. I don't need to "shut down" my sex drive or get mad at myself for having one in the first place. God made my sex drive; I have it for a reason.

If I see a beautiful woman and tell myself, "Oh, if only I were with her," then I am also in lack. I am living in poverty, and God is better than poverty. When I realize how much I already have, I am able to walk in the wealth God has given me. I am full and don't need to take from anyone. I am not lacking; I am not without. Understanding that God is my Shepherd and I lack nothing is both healing and a comfort I desperately need. I don't have to compare myself with anyone or focus on what I don't have, because I am good right where I am.

The biggest thing that has helped me break the chains of loneliness and lust in my life is thankfulness. Thankfulness changes my beliefs and perspective because I am becoming *full of thanks*. When I tell God, "Thank You," I am acknowledging that He has given something to me. It reminds me every time of what I have, which allows me to be truly rich.

I can be thankful for blessings and even for hardships—not for the hardships themselves, but for the beauty of God that lives inside me during hardships. This understanding means that nothing in my life will ever be wasted.

I encourage you to be thankful for the freedoms of being single, for friendships, adventures, and opportunities—and also thank God for the mate He has in store for you.

Activation

And we know that in all things God works for the good of those who love him, who have been called according to his purpose.

Romans 8:28 (NIV)

With that verse in mind, what truths could you thank God for?

Here are a few possibilities:

God, thank You that You love me perfectly and that no negative circumstance in my life can dictate my value. Thank You that I can handle conflict with people. Even if it's difficult and unpleasant or I'm afraid to talk to them, thank You that this is not the end of me. I will survive, and I will love myself during and through the conflict.

9. Friendship and Striving

*Thank You for how You are using this financially
tough time to mold me. Thank You that You
have only blessing in Your heart toward me, and
I know that I will survive and get through this.
Thank You for my friends who are all a gift from
You. Thank You that You meet my needs and
that I don't have to depend upon others' actions
or responses. I don't need other people always
to like me or give me attention.*

*Thank You that there is no fear in love. Thank
You that I am forgiven and there is no
condemnation or shame in You. Thank You for
the desires You have given me, that You've
made me attracted to women and that it's a
beautiful thing. I don't have to try to lower or
crush my desires. Thank You that every struggle
I have with lust was taken care of on the cross
and that I am totally forgiven. Thank You for
what I have learned from past relationships, and
thank You for where you are taking me.*

*Thank You that I don't have to try to please
someone in order to be liked by them.*

I could go on and on. I encourage you to write forty things you
are thankful for and declare them daily. If forty ends up being
too easy, try one hundred. Review them constantly, because
this will change you. It will help take the load off your back
because you will begin to realize that you are truly free from
striving.

Your heavenly Father loves you, and He doesn't need you to be more of something or to try to force something in your own effort. As you give thanks for who you are and what He's doing in your life, you are agreeing with Him, and therefore you'll get to see more clearly what you have, who you are, and who He is.

Single Life Tip

Get lost! When I was single and living in Germany, I was able to explore by getting lost intentionally. I'd just decide to drive down a country road to see where it went, what there was to see, what cool restaurant or castle I'd find, because there was little consequence to getting lost: No one was waiting on me for dinner, no kids to put to bed. While you can, get lost. You'll discover some of the most fascinating things about your world and yourself.

— Jeff

9. Friendship and Striving

10

Ask Her Out

I asked out several of my "friend girls" over the years and received a good number of affirmative replies. Nearly all of them said yes (while most of the women I met online said no), and I didn't take it personally if someone turned me down. It didn't feel good to be turned down, of course, but I made the decision that I wouldn't let it bother me. That was her choice and I could respect it.

I also respected myself for expressing my desire, being honest, and going for it. The more I accepted my desires and expressed them, the less worried I was about getting turned down. Why would I get upset if she said no? If she was so amazing that I wanted to pursue her, then weren't her decisions also amazing? Yes, they were.

Ask your female friends out for coffee or to do fun things you both enjoy. Ask them to join you for that group thing that's coming up. Ask strangers out. Pray about the women around you and who you would like to ask out, and do these things in an honorable way.

In the rest of this chapter, we're going to go over some basic ways you can ask out a woman. Hopefully the steps included in this chapter will fill you with confidence, so you can do what is on your heart to do.

10. Ask Her Out

When You're Asking a Friend to Go Out with You

How in the world do you ask a girl out without making it awkward?

Let's say you want to take one of your friends out for coffee. When you approach her, ask her out with confidence. You don't have to come across so casual that it sounds like you don't want to go, but be direct and straightforward.

You could say something like this: "Hi, _____. I would like to take you out for coffee sometime. How does that sound?" Or you could say, "Hi, _____. I would like to take you out for coffee. Would you have time this week?"

You could even say, "It would be fun to go out for coffee with you sometime. Would ____ (date) work for you?"

If you're texting her the invitation, be clear when you would like to have coffee. Put a date out there, and avoid saying, "Do you want to go out for coffee sometime?" It is easy to say no to an open-ended question or to say yes but then nothing ever happens. I'm not saying it won't work, but it is better for you to be assertive and initiate the time and date.

If she says, "Thank you, but I'm busy at that time," then offer another time. Don't take her answer as a hint that she isn't interested.

If you want to invite a female friend to a group activity, here are a few ways you could do so. You could say something like, "Hey,

____. I'm going hiking at _____ with _____ (these people) on such-and-such date. Want to come with us?"

Or if it makes you feel more comfortable, you could tell your buddy to invite your friend of interest.

If you're planning a group event, it's easy to make a Facebook event and invite people that way. Most girls will come to a group event if they are interested in you or even if they just enjoy your friendship.

Remember, just be yourself and stay comfortable. I know full well how awkward it can be trying to talk to a girl you're interested in. That's okay. Press through the awkwardness and don't analyze it too much. Just because you feel awkward doesn't mean things will always be awkward between the two of you. (That being said, if it continues to be awkward with her even after several conversations, I would take that as a clear sign that being friends with her will be difficult.)

Keep your options open. Just because you invite a girl to a group event doesn't mean you have to talk with her the whole time or exhaust yourself in advance trying to figure out when you "should" talk to her.

When You're Asking a Stranger to Go Out with You

If you want to talk to a girl you don't know, be brave and do it. But *how* do you walk up to a stranger and start talking? Here are a few ways you could do so depending on the context.

10. Ask Her Out

Scenario 1

Let's say you're sitting at a coffee shop and you notice a pretty girl. What do you say to start a conversation?

You could go up to her and ask what she's working on or reading. Tell her what you're doing there, and keep the conversation going by asking her questions: What does she do for work or school? Where is she from? Keep asking questions about a mixture of fun things like travel, hobbies, work, or maybe some things you are passionate about.

After a little while, you can approach the may-I-get-your-number question. You could say something like, "Could I get your number? I'd like to talk more and hang out again." Or "May I have your number? I'd like to take you out to lunch sometime." Or "It would be fun to do this again. I'll give you a call sometime and set something up."

Make it simple and down to earth. There is no need to say, "I'd like to take you on a date." You already had the courage to talk to her and ask for her number, so it should be pretty obvious you're interested.

Another conversation starter is offering to buy her something at the coffee shop. "Hi, I'm _____. What's your name? I'd like to get you _____. Would you like something?"

If she accepts, then go buy the food or drink for her. Or she might want to walk up with you to the counter and pick it out.

Scenario 2

Let's say you're at a group event, and you meet someone who interests you. If you have mutual friends and the chances are high that you'll both be invited to group events in the future, you don't need to rush things. Don't feel pressured to get her number right away, because it is likely you will see her again.

However, if it is unlikely you'll see her again, you should go ahead and ask for her number. Focus on what you want to do and do it. Don't let potentially feeling awkward deter you from action.

Also, don't start playing mind games with yourself. Feeling awkward doesn't mean that asking for her number is wrong or that it isn't "God's will." He gave us free will and He is good; He gives us the desires of our hearts, which means He also *created* the desires of our hearts.

"Do I ask her for her number? What if I don't? Will someone else get to her before me? When will I see her again? Man, I feel nervous!" If you've ever said those things to yourself, smile—you are normal. It is okay to feel nervous and to be uptight, even to feel awkward. But instead of focusing on how awkward you feel, focus on celebrating this girl and how amazing she seems to be. This is easier and way more fun.

Think of asking for her number and showing interest in her as a way of blessing and giving to her. You could say something like,

10. Ask Her Out

"Hey, I'd love to get together sometime for coffee. I don't think I have your number. What is it?"

Text her right then so she has your number too. Make it simple: "Hi, _____. This is _____." Text her again in a few days and invite her to coffee. You could call her as well. The method or formula doesn't always matter. However, if she doesn't answer her phone, don't just hang up—leave a voicemail because a voicemail is bolder. Remember, not answering her phone isn't necessarily a sign that she isn't interested. She might just be busy.

Here is an example of what you could say in a voicemail: "Hi, _____. This is _____. It was great to see you at the _____ on Wednesday (or whenever it was). I want to get together and was wondering if this Saturday morning would work for having breakfast or coffee. Let me know, and I look forward to seeing you again. If Saturday doesn't work, let me know when a better time would be for you. Okay, talk to you soon. Bye." Leaving a voicemail can be super awkward sometimes, so it's okay to be prepared in case she doesn't answer. If you wanted to, you could even practice your message out loud a few times before you called.

If you're nervous, focus on the interest you have in her and how you want to hear more about what is going on in her life. Think about how amazing she is or, simply, that you just want to get to know her more.

As a side note, you don't have to know your level of interest in a woman before asking her out on a date. That is what dates are for. You aren't committing to her; you don't owe her anything and she doesn't owe you anything either. You are completely free just to talk, laugh, and share your stories with each other.

Scenario 3

When is the best time to ask a girl out at church?

If this is a friend of yours, a good time to ask her out is after the service—in the lobby or outside where people are interacting. That is when friends are connecting and making plans for hanging out, so asking a friend out on a date during that time can work well.

"What if she says no and then I'll have to see her every Sunday? Isn't that awkward?" It is only awkward if you make it that way. Most of my dates were women I met at church. They were honored and felt that my interest was a compliment.

You'll have a higher rate of success when you ask out someone you're already friends with; however, there is no harm in asking out a woman you've never met before, and she, too, will likely see it as a compliment.

However, be careful not to ask out strangers too often at your church, work, or wherever else you have community because it isn't good to come across as a player. If you ask out two or three women you don't know and it doesn't seem to be "working," take a break and just focus on being friends with everyone.

10. Ask Her Out

Let's say you and the girl you're interested in serve together at church or you work together—you see each other often. Be thankful for this situation, because you have it easy. You have lots of time to talk and get to know each other. Ask her out for lunch, on a hike, or to do something you both enjoy. Something more active and outdoors can be good. If it feels awkward because you're alone with each other for the first time, focus on all the fun times you've already had with her and how funny she is, how you make her laugh, how amazing her heart is, etc. Put up with the awkwardness. Yes, there are unknowns, but you get to celebrate her and your friendship. Keep doing things with her in group settings as well as spending time together when it is just the two of you.

Most women want to be in a relationship with someone. If your friend is taken or right now isn't a good time for her, let it go because that's the way it's going to be. When you get this answer, continue dialoguing with her and being her friend. Bless her, keep praying for her, and move on.

Here are a few more how-tos from my friend Abram Goff with Moral Revolution.

How to Ask a Girl Out[16]

While attempting to navigate through the dating process, I've found that I'm not alone in my ignorance of how this process is supposed to go down. Many men need courage and many men *just need language* and a healthy example to follow. This is the goal, a quick example and some language to help you out when you see a girl you want to get to know better in three steps: *The Approach, The Question,* and *The Follow Through.*

THE APPROACH: *YOU GOT THIS.*

Take a deep breath. Don't overthink this. Your entire future does NOT hinge on this moment. You're just asking her for coffee or dinner to get to know her better. It's going to be alright. You can do this. You're a good-looking guy, and you're going to make her laugh and smile and bring value to her life.

Remember, relationships are about what you can give to the other person, not what you can get from them. If you're not ready to add value to someone else's life, then you're not ready to date. Assuming, you're ready to give to someone, then go for it and show her a great evening/afternoon. Get out of your head. If she says yes, then you show her how a gentleman should treat a lady. If she says no, you were brave, kicked fear in the

---

[16]Abram Goff, "How to Ask a Girl Out," Moral Revolution, https://moralrevolution.com/how-to-ask-a-girl-out/. Used with permission. (Thanks, Abram!)

face, and broke off passivity. Keep rolling, she just didn't see you with those eyes.

THE QUESTION: *SHORT, SWEET, THEN SILENCE*

I don't know if it's just me, but I've seen "Friends," I know how it's supposed to work. You confidently walk up to a woman you think is attractive and would like to know better and then drop the Joey Tribbiani line: *"How you doin'?"*

I'm joking. While this does show that you've got a good sense of humor and are familiar with 90s pop culture, it's actually never worked for me. At best, I've gotten a good laugh then a period of silence which left me realizing I didn't have a plan for what to say next #awkward. I needed language. So here's what you're going to say, tailor it as needed, but this will give you a start:

IF YOU DON'T KNOW HER:

Find something that you admire about her, besides "she's hot." Notice her smile, her laugh, the way she interacts with others, her shoes, something you like. Approach.

"Hi. I'm sorry, to interrupt, but I just wanted to let you know I really like...(insert honest genuine compliment)."

(She'll say thank you.) Hold out your hand to shake hers and introduce yourself. (She'll tell you her name.)

"I know this may seem a little forward since we just met, but could I take you out for coffee/dinner sometime? I'd love to get to know you better." Easy.

IF YOU ALREADY KNOW HER:

Approach.

"Hey, how's your day/week/month going?"

(Listen to her answer. Respond accordingly. Keep it light and short when she returns the question to you. Don't talk for thirty minutes while awkwardly building up to the question.)

"I've really enjoyed getting to know you and I was wondering if I could take you out for coffee [or dinner?]" Boss. Nailed it.

Here's an important note: if you're nervous after you ask, don't keep talking and explain yourself. Be okay with some silence. This may be a surprise to her and she's running through a lot of thoughts in her head. Just breathe and let her think. Don't feel the need to over-explain yourself. If she's confused, she'll ask. Let her speak.

If you have her phone number, call her. Please don't send her a text asking her out! She wants a man to show up. It's good for us, as men, to be bold and cross that chicken line. I really don't like talking on the phone period, but I want to show women they are worth the phone call. You can use the language given above. Rehearse as much as needed, no shame in that. Just pick up the phone and go for it.

IF YOU GET HER VOICEMAIL:

Don't ask her out over her voicemail. One time, I was so nervous and had rehearsed my words so many times that when her voicemail came on (the shortest voicemail message in the history of the world), I blanked and launched into my speech on her voicemail. Don't do that. It doesn't work. If her voicemail kicks on, keep it short and sweet:

Hey _____, This is _____. I hope you're doing well. I had something I'd love to run past you. Give me a call when you get a chance. My number is _____.

THE FOLLOW-UP: *WHAT TO SAY NEXT*

IF SHE SAYS "YES":

Have two or three ideas and dates in your head. Women like to know you've got a plan and intentions and most of us don't think fast enough to plan when we're nervous. Have two ideas so if the first option is a no-go, you have a back-up plan. P.S. Don't forget to breathe.

Great. How does Monday Night/Thursday Morning/Saturday sound to you? How about the coffee shop on Lincoln Street? Do you like Italian? Mexican? How about Los Tacos on 5th Street?

If it's coffee, set a time you'll meet her. If it's dinner, ask if you can pick her up. Remember, be a gentleman. If she says yes, give her your number and ask her to text you her address, then go clean out your car.

IF SHE SAYS "NO"

Respect the no. Hopefully, she's nice about it. Don't take it personally. It could be that she just got out of a relationship, her grandpa just died, her world is spinning right now, or a hundred other reasons that have nothing to do with you. Don't take it personally and don't beat yourself up. I usually smile and say:

Fair enough. Well, it was a pleasure to meet you. I'm glad we got to talk briefly. I hope you have a wonderful day and it would be great to see you around.

or

That's okay. I really just enjoy getting to know you. If something changes, feel free to let me know. I'd still love to take you out sometime.

HEAR ME ON THIS:

No matter what she says, celebrate yourself. You were bold. You went for it. You gave it a chance and put yourself out there. So much of being a man is showing up, taking a risk, and going for it. You just killed passivity and were courageous. Celebrate yourself for that. After that, enjoy your date or shake it off and find another lovely lady you'd love to get to know better. It doesn't have to be complicated, but going for it and living in the present is always better than living in your head wondering what would have happened.

P.S. If you're a lady reading this, feel free to pass it on to any guys you know or would like to know ;). Guys, if she tagged you in it, go for it. It's going to go well for you.[17]

Keep Going

Every time I have asked a woman out or told her I was interested in her, she thanked me. All of them have respected me for speaking up, because my interest honored them and let them feel pursued. Even when they said no, it always went well for me. Keep that in mind whenever you're working up your nerve to ask someone out.

Even if the worst possible thing happens, and she speaks in a demeaning tone of voice or lets you know she thinks she's above you, you were being a man. You went for what you desired. The desire to pursue a woman you're attracted to and marry her one day is from God. He made you this way, so don't push that desire down.

---

[17] To read more of Abram's material, visit www.abramgoff.com.

Don't put pressure on your "ask." Focus on the fact that you want to do this and that you are simply expressing that desire. Ask your female friends to lunch or coffee, on a walk or hike, for a picnic or group activity, or whatever you want to do that sounds fun and fairly light.

Don't worry that you'll hurt your friendship by doing something alone with this friend who happens to be female. There is actually a greater chance that being honest will *improve* your relationship with her if the alternative is that you're just awkward around her and don't tell her anything.

Remember, it is okay *not* to know if you want to marry her before you ask her on a date. It is even okay not to think she's the most attractive woman you've ever seen. If you just think she's cute and a good friend, that's good enough to ask her out. Attraction can grow, and over time it is possible that the inner beauty and joy can shine through and make her even more beautiful to you.

Don't let the fear of not knowing how much you like her stop you from asking her out and actually discovering how much you like her. Be courageous—move forward despite any fears you may feel, and be intentional or clear about wanting to get to know your friend better by spending time with her.

Activation

This week, plan a group activity with several friends, including your friend of interest.

10. Ask Her Out

If there isn't a girl you're interested in right now, plan the group event anyway and invite several friends. If feasible, open the invitation to your friends' friends as well. This is a great way to meet people.

Try to put together an event about once a month, and be sure to go to the events you are invited to. Have fun!

Single Life Tip

Don't misinterpret loneliness with love. You control your own happiness.

— Daron

11
Masturbation: Taking Matters into Your Own Hands

This is a book written for singles, so of course there's going to be a chapter on masturbation. But it probably isn't what you expect.

As you may already know, there isn't a single verse in Scripture that says masturbation is a sin. In fact, the Bible doesn't talk about it at all. Unfortunately, many people use shame in an attempt to curb the younger generation's sexual urges. It's like they think that shame actually has the power to help people.

Personally, I am not for masturbation, but it isn't because I grew up hearing from all the adults that it's a sin, wrong, or a shameful act. I say no to it because it robs me of being a powerful person. It takes away intimacy with actual people and keeps me from facing my pain, anxiety, and loneliness. It merely numbs these things instead. I have a clearer mind, stronger conviction in my life, and many other positives because I choose not to masturbate.

I didn't always feel this way. It actually took me several years to realize how masturbation affects men. I used to do it once a week and sometimes more often. When I was in junior high and high school, I masturbated sometimes more than once a day. I thought I was the only one doing this and wondered if my friends were. As I got older, there were times when I went months or almost a full year without masturbating, which really isn't anything to brag about.

11. Masturbation: Taking Matters into Your Own Hands

I'm telling you all of this because I know the struggles and challenges. I know the drive and the urges. I'm a "Palmer," for Pete's sake.

But here's what I do that may help you. When I'm feeling horny, I call a friend just to talk and share how I'm doing. I get off of all social media and my computer. I go to the bathroom. I write in my journal, thanking God and worshiping Him. Sometimes I exercise right where I am; I get down and do push-ups or squats. I have found that exercise really helps release the tension I feel. All those hormones do not have to run my life or control me.

In times like this when I pray, I don't cry out about how weak I am and focus on how difficult this challenge is. Doing those things actually *reinforces* how weak I am, which makes it easier to act out.

I don't have to stay in a weak mindset in order for God to act. This is actually my issue, not God's. It isn't His fault that I'm struggling, and it isn't His responsibility to keep me from sinning. I am not a robot. Self-control is a fruit of the spirit because all of us need it.

What are the benefits of staying "sober"? Having real emotions, better connection with yourself, more confidence, and more joy. You will feel stronger as a person, not weaker. A big benefit of not masturbating is more confidence in dealing with conflicts and stress. The thing you want to do to relieve stress (masturbate) actually creates more stress because you won't be as confident or have as strong a conviction for what you think or want to say.

Masturbation is often used to numb pain. By not masturbating, you will be able to process the pain better and get over it more quickly.

Also, you will feel *real* because you are living in reality with real people, and you'll experience real emotions based on real things. You'll feel better because each day that you don't masturbate, you become stronger by resisting. And then, my friend, your desire to masturbate will begin to decline, and your brain will want to do healthy activities that make you feel good. You'll want to do more adventurous things and be more creative, funny, relaxed, and bold. You will be freer to share what's on your mind.

I like to be happy, and masturbation actually causes me to lose peace. So then I try to be happy to cover up the fact that I'm feeling lame; I fake smile and pretend I'm doing great. Again, I don't do this to cover up shame—just my feelings of being lame. But isn't that lame by itself? It would be better for me to go get real peace and joy instead.

Many men think that masturbating has no ill effects on them. However, if you try going without, you'll see the improvements. Living in reality is always more healthy.

Honestly, it comes down to this: Running from pain or stress is not being a mature adult. Children do this, not adults. When I numb myself to pain, I am not living in reality. Worse, I am not being present in my situation. I am not being fully me and allowing God to heal me completely. That, in my opinion, is the biggest reason not to masturbate. When I "medicate" my pain, I am not allowing God to comfort me and I am distancing myself from His touch in my life. I am also robbing myself of really feeling my emotions and allowing myself to go through them and come out on the other side actually healed.

Who Cares?

Who really cares whether or not you masturbate?

This issue is only important if you want to live life to its fullest, if you want a closer relationship with God, and if you want to be a powerful person and have intimacy with other people. This does not mean you will be a more *valuable* person or that God will love you more if you give up masturbating. However, it does mean you will experience love in a greater way and have less stress and more power.

I don't mean to sound strict with this topic. What I'm doing is presenting an opportunity for you to feel more, to be more alive, to be stronger and more powerful, to have a clear conscience and more peace, and to take greater risks and pursue the three main things we've been talking about in this book: freedom, manhood, and women.

Don't give up masturbating out of religious duty. Give it up so you can walk in peace and security—so you can walk through the pain and not keep holding on to it. The desire to masturbate will let up. It will lessen with time as you go without.

Porn, Again

In my struggle with masturbation, porn has also tried to be my companion. As a freshman in high school, I started looking at pictures of women in photography stores. My appetite grew to renting R- or unrated movies, which I'd watch late at night after coming home from work. In my early twenties when the internet became more popular, I would watch very slow-moving videos of women undressing.

It was definitely an escape for me. An escape from feeling inadequate, from performing, from insecurity, from boredom, and the list went on. But over time, this is what I discovered: Porn was and is a lie. The smiles and comforting looks and the momentary pleasure of seeing the female body revealed a need I had, yet these moments always left me feeling terrible. They took something from me. I was robbed of strength as well as courage, righteousness, peace, love, power, and my manhood itself.

I've been trying to find freedom from lusting after women and watching dirty videos, including porn, since I was a teenager. Over time I've come to understand that it is a process. I can say that I am growing in this area and that I lust after women far less than I have in the past. I don't have a perfect track record, but it is improving. I am more in touch with my emotions and making better decisions; I am reaching out and am completely open and honest with my fiancée about this struggle.

Porn is an epidemic in America, and we can see its effects daily: depression, social anxiety, insecurity, and a lack of desire for a real relationship, among other destructive things. Looking at porn to medicate your pain is similar (not in degree but in principle) to being really hungry but, instead of satisfying your hunger, you decide *not* to eat. In a similar way, porn doesn't satisfy. Porn hurts us; it never helps us. You may think that if you weren't in pain, you wouldn't want to look at porn, but in my opinion, looking at porn is actually causing you additional pain and making your other pain worse. Like masturbation, porn doesn't allow you to deal with your pain.

Not only is looking at porn sinful, but it devalues women and turns you into a wet slice of bread. It creates a reaction in your brain called dopamine, which is like a drug. So looking at porn becomes a cheap fix, yet it is costly. A healthier way to experience a high in life is by going on adventures, taking risks, exercising, pursuing hobbies, etc. After I exercise, I don't even think about looking at porn and am not tempted.

When you look at porn, you make it that much more challenging to be a strong man, to be thankful, and to enjoy what God has put in your life: the outdoors, people, relationships, your career. It becomes much harder to have peace, confidence, rest and comfort—and to pursue a woman! It is a big fat lie from the devil that porn will comfort you or that it doesn't hurt you or the people in your life.

The key is to run from temptation—don't fight it. Trying to fight off temptation will wear you down, and then once you're tired and your best defenses are starting to sag, it's easier than ever to give into temptation, simply because you are tired of fighting.

Running from temptation means avoiding practical things that make it easy to view porn. If media is an area of trouble for you, don't try to be macho and leave lots of tempting media around you—run from the temptation. If you need to add Covenant Eyes (an app that restricts browsers) to your computer and phone, do it. If you need to remove all internet access from your phone, do it. If that doesn't work, put your phone outside your room at night so it's not a temptation. Get a real alarm clock. Block sites that are a temptation, even Youtube. Don't worry about whether or not your friends know you're blocking a site. Your freedom is something you have to fight for. Do what you need to do to be safe.

Have accountability partners, and purposefully share with each other how all of you did this past week. But more than just reporting your failures, encourage each other and be accountable to greatness. If you are a Christ follower, a child of God, you are destined for greatness. You are spotless and blameless and holy, so point each other toward who you truly are.

Focusing on sin doesn't allow God's forgiveness to impact you deeply, nor does it offer you the grace you need to obey Him. His grace is sufficient for you. Read Romans 6 and Ephesians 1–2. No matter how many years, or even decades, you've looked at porn, you can stop and retrain your brain to enjoy real intimacy, real connection, actual excitement and joy, and confidence around beautiful women. You'll be able to relate to your friends and coworkers more, and you'll be more creative, productive, and the list goes on.

Perhaps you aren't looking at "porn," but you're playing video games filled with barely clothed women or lusting after models you find online. Perhaps you're constantly watching the women all around you, hoping they bend over so you can see their breasts. Be aware of what's going on in your heart, and do what you need to do to find freedom.

It is possible to turn your eyes from a situation before it occurs. I know that things happen, sometimes without warning. But you can control where you look after that moment.[18]

This is my prayer for you:

> *Father God, I pray that my readers who are struggling with masturbation, porn, or lust would experience a filling of peace. Open their hearts to being authentic about their pain and needs, and help them to tell You and a close friend about these things when the need arises. Thank You that You meet us where we are, and we don't have to be perfect or all put together in advance. We are actually comforted by You with real and lasting peace when we shed our darkness to step into Your light. Amen.*

Activation

Read Colossians 2:16–23, and don't follow a rule just because it is a rule. That line of reasoning won't work for you in the long run.

---

[18] For help in overcoming a porn addiction, visit www.freedomu.net.

Surrender this issue to God. Give Him the lie that you must feel pleasure all the time and never feel pain. Turn your sexual frustration into something more productive. Do the fun things you've been wanting to do or wishing you had time to do. Call that friend you haven't talked to in a long time. Learn that hobby, work out, make something, write, clean, read, listen to excellent music. Every time you find yourself being tempted, see what you can do instead that is productive, fun, exciting, or perhaps involves risk. Get your game plan on paper and have it ready before crunch time. Make sure to do something you *want* to do and don't focus on avoiding the thing you don't want to do.

If you do masturbate or look at porn, confess what happened to God. Also, be sure to tell someone about it (Jas. 5:16) because this helps remove shame. Don't let anything be hidden, but bring it into the light so it can be revealed and healed.

Tell God you're sorry and that the next time you find yourself in a similar situation, you want to turn to Him for comfort instead. Don't beat yourself up because this actually weakens you; you are despising yourself. Come into agreement with God's forgiveness and forgive yourself, because He has.

Remember, you are not above God. You are not the judge, and you are not more special than the cross. Your sins are not too great for Him to forgive, nor are they so huge that He will turn His back on you and cease to accept you as a son. Let go of your self-hatred and self-punishment. Surrender to His goodness and His thoughts towards you.

11. Masturbation: Taking Matters into Your Own Hands

Pray this prayer:

> *God, I surrender my sex drive to You. I give up any sense of entitlement I feel to have sex and choose to see it as a gift saved for the intimacy and covenant of marriage. I want to trust You with my feelings and my sex drive. I welcome Your presence, Your comfort, Your Word, and Your intimacy with me. Thank You for all the amazing things I can do with my time that make me feel alive, like a real man, and powerful. I choose to seek You more than I seek anything else. Thank You, Father God, for Your grace that enables me to be whole and real. Amen.*

Single Life Tip

Never say no to a road trip. Practice generosity. Savor beauty. Do your dishes every night. Pray for miracles until they come. Learn to dance well. Learn to grieve well. Invest your time, energy, and money in places that will bear fruit for the long haul. Celebrate. Dream. Listen. Worship until you've lost track of anything else that had ever seemed important.

— Christina

12
Giving It All Up

Several years ago I attended a wedding in Portland, where I met up with a woman I had a big-time crush on, but she made me nervous. Her parents were well-known authors, and she also was widely known and had a following. At the wedding, I actually found myself wishing I were someone else, someone she would be interested in. I wanted her to like me so much that I froze, thinking only of how I wanted to be with her. In all honesty, it was a disgusting feeling. I didn't even have a good time with her on the dance floor because I wanted to be accepted so badly that I forgot to accept myself. I danced a little bit and then stepped away to speak with a few friends before leaving the reception. Overall, the event ended up being pretty awful.

In a time when I really wished to be married, I was single and at a wedding. I put an enormous amount of pressure on myself to hit it off well with this girl, a person I didn't *really* know. How was putting pressure on myself supposed to make me cooler and enable me to have a good time?

Why do we do that to ourselves? We think we'll be happier when we're married, so we apply pressure to ourselves to go out and find a wife.

We want our own families; we want to share our lives with someone. Those are good things, right? Yet many times, we end up feeling desperate. And desperation has nothing in common with loving someone and being unselfish.

For us to represent how we will live as married men, it is in our best interest to start practicing now. If we want to be giving toward the women we will marry, how can we represent our hearts to give while we are still single? One key way we can reveal the kind of husbands we will be one day is by choosing not to be demanding now. In other words, instead of being desperate to find this special person, we choose to surrender. This doesn't mean we stop wanting a relationship. It means we commit this desire to the Lord. We give it to Him.

After moving to Redding, I was interested in a friend of mine who was not interested in me in return. I'd been matched with her on several dating sites before I even moved to Redding, and I had a crush on her but didn't know her at all. We ended up meeting in person at a party, and I saw her again at a few group events. As we started hanging out, I found myself caught up in the fantasy of being in a relationship with her. But she wanted to remain just friends and told me this quite clearly.

That was hard for me to hear because I had put her up on a pedestal and painted a strong internal picture of what it would look like to be with her. In the end, I had to give up my desire to be with her. It took me about two months to do this, but I had to because it was eating me up.

Have you ever heard someone say, "Rest in the Lord," and it made you start wondering how you're supposed to get anything done if you're "resting"? Or perhaps a well-meaning person has told you to "just trust in the Lord." Does that mean you're supposed to sit around and not do anything? Are you supposed to trust God to put food on the table for you? Pay your bills? What are *you* supposed to do, and what is *God* supposed to do? How do you trust God for a wife and still look for one at the same time?

Resting or trusting in God doesn't mean we don't do any work. It means we do our part without any fear. That is the key. We work toward what we want without fear of punishment, rejection, failure, or love being withheld. Striving is what happens when we work toward what we want but are motivated by all those gross things I just mentioned.

Being a good man who is at rest means I don't put pressure on myself to have it all together. And pursuing a woman while at rest doesn't mean I stand along the wall and watch everyone else dance. It means I go after my desires, and I go after the woman I want to without fear of failure, rejection, or not being adequate. I may be able to sense those fears, but I move forward anyway. That is what courage is— moving forward even if you are afraid.

Being a man means you treat yourself with love while you are pursuing a woman. It doesn't mean you kick yourself into becoming a better man.

That is what giving it all up looks like. It is the reason people say, "When you stop trying to meet someone, you will." Ha! Whatever. If we take that "formula" at face value, it almost sounds like we have to shut down our desires before we'll meet someone. That saying can actually push us toward carelessness.

But I think the true intention of the saying is to remove pressure. It is supposed to help us not to strive or worry about meeting the right person. When we are no longer worrying, we are free to be the strong, amazing men we are.

Activation

Is there a relationship you need to "give up"? I don't mean a relationship where you need to stop trying but one where you need to stop trying to be in control. Or stop trying to control her. Spend some time with God and ask Him that question.

Afterward pray this prayer:

> Lord, I choose to trust You for a wife. I pray for peace that surpasses all my own ways, my own understanding, my desires, and even my timetable. Thank You, Lord, that You do make all things beautiful in Your time. Fill me with grace to trust You and to pursue women with love and not from the fear of missing out. Thank

You, Father, that this is possible with You.
Amen.

Single Life Tip

Don't wait for anything or anyone. Just say yes. When you say yes, the possibilities are wide open; your heart and soul are open to receiving joy from an experience.

— Chelsea

12. Giving It All Up

13

Interview with Jack and Faith Vu

I was able to interview my friends Jack and Faith in the beginning stages of their dating relationship, and I found their answers to be deep and insightful. They married a short time ago—which tells me they know at least a *little* of what they're talking about.

What have you learned from past unhealthy relationships?

Faith: The first thing I learned is that intimacy needs to match commitment level. In this past relationship, we were intimate, but we didn't have commitment. We were doing all the emotional and physical things of a close relationship, but it didn't have the commitment. As your commitment grows, so does your intimacy.

Another thing I learned is that you need to surround yourself with community because oftentimes you don't see things that they do see. Input is really healthy for a relationship. My friends and family were confused about our relationship. I wasn't open to advice because I knew that my relationship was unhealthy and needed to change, but I didn't want it to.

Peers that don't know how to do life well don't know how to confront either. So it's good to surround yourself with leaders that have authority to speak into your life and people that you respect, like spiritual parents. Having people in your life that you can submit to is important.

Was it stressful to be in that kind of relationship?

Faith: It was a stressful relationship because it was confusing and I couldn't talk to anyone, so it was like a dead end.

I learned that we do a lot of things out of fear without knowing it, so it's important to have people that see our blind spots. Being told, "You're acting out like this because you don't want to be alone," or "You are doing this because you don't know your worth," or something substantial like that would have been very helpful.

Surround yourself with people that are more self-aware than you are.

Jack: If you are in a rut, you attract people like you. It sucks—it's hard to find people that are healthy. Tell people that you want to be intentional with them.

We spent a lot of time with groups in the beginning. When you are in a group, you have more time to be comfortable. I'm all for "doing friendship" while building a friendship. It's good to have that accountability with other people—and have the focus be on other people too.

Faith: The Holy Spirit always tells you what is going on, and if you want to, you can listen to this.

Jack: I used to not have a close relationship with God, and it was based on my performance. I thought I had to be "good" in order to approach Him.

Faith: God is such a good pursuer of our hearts. Having a good relationship with God allows us to have a good relationship with others. My relationships with others are a reflection of my relationship with God. Include Him in every decision.

Our lives are a reflection of Him and His nature. God wants to be included in every decision.

Know that God is actually a really good Father. Knowing He won't hand me a stone if I ask for bread gives me confidence that I can come to Him honestly, knowing that His goodness is a foundation. It was like He said to me, "Tell Me what you want and not just what you need." So I did and then I met Jack.

Jack: Learn how to do relationships well. For example, learn how to confront people and work things out instead of having fallouts because you don't want to stick it out. Learn how to build friendships with friends first. If you don't know how to build vulnerability and trust with your friends, then you can't do that with your spouse.

What you find for guys is that we'll take our need to be valuable from the woman instead of knowing who we are in God. This can be turned codependent as well.

Learn how to communicate. It's a learned skill. See where there is a conflict and stay in that relationship, even if it is uncomfortable. Relationships end when people don't say what they are feeling. If you assume to know what the other person is saying, then it makes you an ass.

What's your advice for early dates?

Jack: Tell the girl you would like to take her out on a date. Be very clear. Do you want to be friends for a while and then ask her out? Not necessarily. It can work to just go up to a girl and ask her.

But most of the time, I think it would be too forward to just ask a girl out on a date the first time you see her. I saw Faith across the room, and I walked over to her and started talking. I got her Facebook, and I created a group game night event and then got her number from that. Then I called her the next day. It's not a formula—you have to feel it out.

But if it's the only time you think you are going to see the girl, then ask for that date.

Faith: It was awesome because there were many places for us to see each other with each other's circle of friends. Make your intentions clear. Being super brave helps women know where you are at.

Judd: It seems to be a challenging point for guys.

Jack: It's as awkward as you make it. Ask them out and if they say no, then move on. It's that "ask" that gives you that frog in your throat. Guys need a season to ask every pretty girl out—it builds that confidence.

I know of a lot of guys that struggle with that, but we are the ones that are risking first. God made us for this.

Judd: What about you, Faith? What's it like being a girl and waiting for a guy that you like to make that move? Or how do you show that you're interested without being too forward?

Faith: That's interesting. Me and my girlfriends talk about that all the time—the new rule of the girl being powerful, even to the point of proposing marriage. I am very conventional, and I believe it's the guy that needs to do the pursuing. It's a reflection of Jesus pursuing the bride.

What if a girl likes someone, but he doesn't like her? The question is, should she wait for him to pursue her? If the guy actually doesn't like her right now—does that mean it won't work? If you need to persuade him, then it probably won't work out. But then sometimes it does work out—it's not a cookie-cutter answer.

Maybe he does like you, but he isn't man enough to ask. I would say that if he is not man enough to ask, then he is not man enough to be your boyfriend. But some girls don't care about that and they just ask.

Jack: How do you want your story to read? That's what I ask myself, personally. It's your preference; it's not a cookie-cutter thing. If people don't want that standard, then they are missing out.

Do girls talk to each other? Do they say things like, "I like this guy, but I wish he would pursue me"?

Faith: Girls talk a lot. They consult each other for advice. Not all of them do this, but a lot of them do. We talk about it. For me, I talked with my housemates about Jack and told them he wanted to do group things and asked me to accompany him. I was super open with my housemates and told them what I wanted from them and what I needed. I invited feedback about anything that wasn't healthy.

Sometimes girls can be unhelpful because we are hopeless romantics and sometimes live in fantasy. Living in reality is helpful too.

Jack: Peel back and zoom out. There is so much grace. We don't know how to do relationships; we haven't seen it done in a healthy way, but there is so much grace on it. Of course you are going to make mistakes. When we learn something, we think, *Oh man. We have to do this perfect.* We use God as a Band-Aid. It's like, "Oh, I am waiting on God," or "I'm waiting on my season." But you don't know what's going to come out unless you start.

Judd: I see dating or relationships like a job. You make a mistake and then you learn from it. I can get so hard on myself when it's better just to have fun with it and learn from things. I failed there because I was really wanting to be loved.

Also I had to learn what my type is. Do I want someone that is quieter than me, or do I want someone more outgoing? What is it that I want?

Faith: Relationships are always going to be messy. You have two people learning how to do life in the process of life.

What do you want to say to readers who are dealing with shame?

Jack: I would say first—get your mind right. Get right with God. We need other people to speak that truth into us.

Vulnerability kills shame. Be open with another person and share what happened. We need to know that we are enough.

Faith: And you need someone that will kick your butt too and say you are way better than that. If you made a mistake that involved another person, tell them you are sorry that you did this. Sharing everything brings it to the light and removes shame. Whenever you are feeling shame, speak it.

Jack: Do not isolate.

Activation

Write down some of the points you've learned from past relationships and how you are going to handle your next relationship. Thank God for all you are learning, and ask Him to show you the areas He wants you to grow in.

Write down what He reveals to you, and thank Him for the grace to do these things in your next relationship.

Single Life Tip

Stop making it all about you. As men, we need to look outside ourselves and be generous with what we are and who we are. Women need us just as much as we need them.

— Justin

14
Right Here, Right Now

"Whoa," my mom cautioned from the passenger seat.

"Mom, it's okay," I replied.

"I am not comfortable with you following so closely to other cars."

I backed off from the car in front of me.

Silence.

"You need to slow down. Please keep it within five of the speed limit."

"Mom, I'm driving with the flow of traffic."

"I'm not comfortable with you driving this fast."

My mom is used to my dad's driving. He's a smooth operator, and all his driving changes are gentle and gradual; he drives just above the speed limit and has been doing so ever since I can remember. That's how my mom likes it.

At the time of this conversation, however, I was young and, let's say, more of a *spontaneous* driver. My mom once had me pull to the side of the road so she could drive because the way I drove was not relaxing for her.

As I got older, I determined to master the skill of driving with my parents whenever we went somewhere together. To do this, I had to respect how they wished to be driven. First, this meant driving with more space between my car and the one in front of me and not being in a hurry to get to our destination. Second, it meant driving the same speed and not "accidentally" ten miles per hour over the speed limit. (This typically happened because I wasn't paying attention to the speedometer.) I practiced making smoother lane changes and began to look farther ahead, so I would be better prepared for slowdowns or merging lanes.

Finding my driving acceptable, my parents began to feel more comfortable in the car with me. I took pride in gaining their comfort and peace.

What does driving a car have to do with dating? Nothing at all. But this story highlights my point: Doing the right things *now* will lead to doing greater things later. Respecting others now— your housemates, your family, the girls you are dating, your coworkers and parents—will eventually lead to your future girlfriend and wife placing her trust in you later on.

How you treat those around you now, and especially how you treat your mother, is a direct indicator of how you will treat your dates and future wife. Though I think I've treated my mom with respect throughout my life, the way I handled her driving preferences was a reflection of an area of respect that I needed to grow in.

Respecting someone's preferences at the specific point where they differ from yours clearly reveals what your respect level looks like. It puts it right up in your face. The more you respect the women in your life, the more you will be interested in asking them out and being in an actual relationship.

You may think you already respect women, and you may be a cool guy with lots of female friends, but the true test of respect comes when women have a different opinion than you do or when they want something that you feel isn't a big deal. Like my mother and my driving. When this occurs, do you laugh at them and what they are saying, or do you respect their comfort level, even though it is totally different than yours?

Ephesians 5:21–27 (TPT) is a popular passage about love and respect between a husband and wife:

> Out of reverence for Christ be supportive of each other in love.
>
> For wives, this means being supportive to your husbands like you are tenderly devoted to our Lord, for the husband provides leadership for the wife, just as Christ provides leadership for his church, as the Savior and Reviver of the body. In the same way the church is devoted to Christ, let the wives be devoted to their husbands in everything.
>
> And to the husbands, you are to demonstrate love for your wives with the same tender devotion that Christ demonstrated to us, his bride. For he died for us, sacrificing himself to make us holy and pure, cleansing us through the showering of the pure water of the Word of

> God. All that he does in us is designed to make
> us a mature church for his pleasure, until we
> become a source of praise to him—glorious and
> radiant, beautiful and holy, without fault or
> flaw.

What do I do with this passage if I'm single? Do I disregard it because I am not married, or is there an application for me right here, right now, toward the ladies in my life?

I would like to propose that even when I am single, I can live in a "laying myself down for her" way in everyday situations: in conversations, interactions, and on dates. What do I get out of this since I'm not married? Is it just me being a martyr? Not exactly. I get to practice laying myself down for others. I get to "die" to myself with women, friends, authorities, family, and vulnerable adults and seniors. And the rewards I receive for doing so are beautiful things like maturity, becoming "radiant," and enjoying being Christlike. Jesus is freedom, which means that laying down my life for others actually makes me *freer* than I was before.

I get to be unselfish and let Jesus be everything to me, so He can flow into me and overflow toward others. The more I practice being a true friend and acting and communicating out of love, the more I will be able to do these things when I am married. Learning how to do these things now is a much better plan than choosing to live for myself in the moment and having to learn how to die to myself later, after I get married.

A basketball player doesn't sit at home playing video games about basketball in order to get ready for a game. No, he practices playing basketball so that when the game starts, he's ready to play ball and bring it. In everyday life, "practicing" dying to self looks like being patient, being a friend, letting go of her when she doesn't want to stay in touch, praying blessing on her, and praying for the best for her. It means being a good listener and asking good questions. It means being thoughtful and gentle.

Interestingly enough, dying to self also means taking risks.

Does that surprise you? When we hear about "dying to self," many of us automatically assume it means being a passive rollover or a boring person. No, my friend. It means not worrying about what others think of you because you are alive in Christ. You are dead to acting out selfishly, dead to fear of failure, and alive to being joyful and having freedom from shame and condemnation. You're alive to be bold and take a risk—alive to be yourself.

A risk could mean anything. It could mean saying to a pretty woman you just met, "I would like to spend time with you. I would like to take you out to coffee. I would like to go on a walk with you." Or whatever else you want to do. Why is this dying to yourself? Because it is going after what you want and expressing the will of God in you. It is being vulnerable.

I see many guys who are great at sports or at their jobs, but they aren't great or comfortable around beautiful women. If you can relate to this, I have a question for you: What did you do to become good at your job or that sport or hobby? Or how are you able to volunteer or lead at church? Take your answers to those questions and apply them to taking risks with the woman you are interested in.

Practice. Study. Just go for it. You wanted that job; you did research and applied yourself, and you took a risk by interviewing. You went to school or obtained the license or certificate to qualify for the job. You expressed your desire for the job by contacting the company and asking for an interview. You put yourself out there.

How can you use the same skills and methods for taking a risk with a desirable woman? Maybe you could become her friend, get to know her first, and then ask her out on a date. If you just met her, maybe you could talk with her for several minutes and ask her for her phone number so you can arrange a date for another time. This all takes courage and putting yourself out there.

When you apply for a job or head to an interview, do you think confidently? Yes, you do. You even think confidently about a job that may be a step up for you. That you got your current job shows your level of experience. Or perhaps you were hired because of a degree or a connection you have through a friend or family member. Is pursuing a woman you don't know very well that much different? Obviously, there are *some* differences in this analogy, but what it takes to develop a "relationship" with the job you want can be similar to pursuing a woman. You're getting to know each other and seeing if this would be a good fit. You're serving her. You take risks by having an interview. What if she ends up not "hiring" you? That's okay. You just thank her and move on.

Does it mean you are a loser if she says no? Not at all. Yes, it can be awkward, and being turned down can hurt the ego. But—you asked her. You expressed yourself and you went for it. Be proud of that. You took a risk and practiced, and now you get to move on and try something else.

There are many reasons a woman may not be interested in you. Some of them are personal and some are not, and it's okay either way. If you think she's amazing but she isn't into you, it means you wouldn't be a good match. Respect her decision and remember that if she's truly amazing, then her decision not to go out with you needs to be amazing too.

There is someone for you, someone you will "click" with, and it won't be like pulling a tooth to talk with her.

God wants you to have the fulfillment of the desires He gave to you, so you need to be honest about your desires and pursue them because you are made in His image. Your desires and influence in this world reflect His nature and bring Him glory— and to you they bring joy.

Activation

Think about your relationship with your mom. Are there any areas that need reconciliation, forgiveness, or peace? Is there anything you need to apologize for? If something comes to mind, I encourage you to contact her and start by apologizing for where you were wrong, and also tell her how much you appreciate her.

If you haven't already done so, it could be helpful to share with her any areas where she hurt you, as she may not be aware of how certain things affected you. But before jumping off that cliff, ask her if she is open to hearing this from you. Also ask God for wisdom in when and how to share these things.

If you aren't able to contact her, search your heart to see if there is any bitterness toward your mom. If there is, write a letter to her forgiving her for anything she did that caused you pain, and also apologize for any areas where you acted in a hurtful way against her. After completing the letter, if you feel you've forgiven her, burn the letter as an act of closure and forgiveness.

Thank God for His forgiveness and for every positive thing you can think of about your mom.

Single Life Tip

Speak courage into others. Dive into the depths of what it means to be loved by God. Love Him deeply and then love whoever is next to you.

— Christina

15
Red Flags, Bells, and Whistles

When I was twenty-two, I was living in Minneapolis and having the time of my life as I attended college and really got to know my relatives who lived close by in Wisconsin.

Nearly two hundred relatives on both sides of my family lived within about fifty miles of each other. The Palmer and Nelson families have a rich heritage in that area. When I was growing up, I'd always enjoyed visiting Grandma and Grandpa, aunts, uncles, and cousins for Christmas or summer vacations. So I thought it would be awesome to move out there, finish up college, and spend time really getting to know my relatives, because family is big to me.

Not too long after I moved out there, I was in a college-age group at a thriving church in Minneapolis and met a girl I will call Brenda. One night I had Brenda, her best friend, and the best friend's boyfriend over for a movie and pizza, and Brenda and I laughed together more than her friends did. We really hit it off. After being friends for about two weeks, we started dating. She was my first girlfriend.

We had lots of fun together. We made each other laugh, held hands and kissed, and did the usual progression of spending more and more time together and visiting with each other's families.

I didn't really know what I was doing. I just liked her and kept moving things forward. Did I love her? I wasn't sure and started wondering what it felt like to love someone enough to propose. As a romantic, I enjoyed being in a relationship; I also enjoyed her affection and the way she liked me. We were physically connected as well. We didn't have sex, but we did fondle each other and make out like crazy. We slept together in the same bed a few times, and I began to feel guilty about how physically involved I was with her.

Also I knew we weren't on the same page spiritually. I had a stronger and more personal relationship with God than I thought she did, but I felt like I could help her in this area so I didn't let the difference bother me.

After about eight months of dating, I was asking myself marriage questions. I was and still am big into counseling and getting everything out in the open, so we started going to pre-engagement counseling, which just made us even more attracted to each other.

I planned out a private proposal at my apartment. I had nice plates and glasses, champagne, and good Chinese food, along with our "theme song" ready to go on the CD player. When I got down on my knees and asked Brenda to marry me, I slipped the diamond ring on her finger and she said yes. We were in love, and it was wonderful for both of us.

Perhaps you know where the rest of this story is going. Maybe it sounds a lot like your story.

We went to pre-marriage counseling shortly after that at another church. This round of counseling was much more in depth, talking about our backgrounds, baggage, which personality differences work well together and which personalities can clash with others, finances, gender roles, and other important topics. This was where I began to feel concerned about some of our key differences.

Then Brenda started doing things I wasn't expecting. She began reacting with anger—strong anger—over small things. For instance, one morning in the car I realized I had food in my teeth and tried to fix it, and she grew livid.

"Five-year-olds can take care of themselves," she said. "I'm not going to marry someone that can't take care of himself."

Wow. I couldn't believe it. We had a few more super-heated interactions, and over the course of several months, these "discussions" started to douse the flame of my fire for this woman. When she left on a college band trip to Disneyland for a week, I felt relieved that I had a break from her.

I shared with my parents how I felt, and they answered that it sounded like I was scared or had anxiety about marrying her. That made sense to me. So when Brenda returned from her band trip, I asked her, "Would you consider postponing the wedding date and getting some one-on-one counseling?"

She refused, telling me it was either this date or not at all.

To this day, I'm still not exactly sure what happened with Brenda. She seemed to change after we were engaged. A month after I proposed, I found I didn't trust her like I used to and didn't have as much peace.

For a week, I went back and forth about breaking things off. She and I had some intense conversations about our relationship and what we expected out of it. One night I called my dad to talk about how things were going, and again he gave me quality feedback on how I was feeling. In the end, I broke off the engagement after two months.

It was the hardest thing I had ever done. Brenda wept openly and I felt horrible. She gave the ring back to me, and her best friend came and picked her up from my apartment. I felt gutted, yet I also knew it was the right thing to do. It was the best decision for her and the best decision for me.

Knowing I was sticking up for what I needed to do and making a decision that was going to be the best for both of us gave me a strong sense of integrity. If we had pushed through what was happening between us and gotten married anyway, it likely would have been a horrendous situation for us both.

The concerns I mentioned and a general lack of peace are called *red flags*. They are signs of danger, and they are worthy of attention. Red flags tell you something is wrong. They are like the human nervous system that loudly responds if you touch something too hot: "This is painful! Don't do this because it will hurt you."

I am very thankful, not to mention relieved, that I paid attention to the red flags with Brenda and broke up with her. Yes, it was the most painful and difficult thing I had done up to that point, but it was the best decision I could have made.

About ten months later, Brenda and I met for coffee, and she thanked me for breaking up with her, saying she'd realized that she wasn't ready to get married at that point. Man, that was nice to hear.

If we wish to do so, red flags can be ignored. We can get caught up in all the bells and whistles of engagement and planning a wedding and choose not to listen to what the red flags are saying.

Or we can pay attention to the warning signs and save ourselves the pain of a potential divorce or a terrible marriage.

The Trouble with Infatuation

I explain infatuation as being in love with love, not with the other person. It is possible to be infatuated with getting married because it is the biggest desire you have and you've had it for most of your life. If you are infatuated with marriage, your desire to find somebody and get married could begin to control you and potentially lead you into an unhealthy situation.

If you find yourself in this situation, take a step back. Focusing on all the hype of getting married won't produce a lasting connection with the person you care for. If in the end the two of you are not a good match, you can face the pain of breaking up now or the greater pain of getting married to someone who plants some big red flags inside you.

Infatuation, being in love with love, can spark relationships between two people who likely never would have been involved with each other otherwise. Sometimes we can find ourselves in a relationship with someone who isn't a good match for us because we wanted to be in a relationship so badly, or because it feels good to make her laugh and have her attention and adoration. If you're in a relationship that is starting to show clear red flags, this is a good time to ask yourself some important questions:

- What do I actually like about her?
- How am I contributing to this relationship, and why do I want to be with her?
- What purpose and passions do we share?
- What are we heading toward in life?

To have a relationship based in reality, it is essential to be together in real-life situations and around all your friends. That is what Melissa and I were able to do. Now my fiancée, she and I began just as friends in a crowd. Because of this, I was able to see her in "her environment," without her trying to impress me or be someone she wasn't. I was also able to be who I normally am, showing her how I acted around different friends and giving her a chance to learn about me. We were able to build trust with each other and place our interest in each other, not in the fact that we were in a relationship.

When possible, go on group dates with friends and even family members. This doesn't have to be an awkward, meet-the-parents kind of scenario. Make it natural, and let your date see who you are in these environments. Later find out what your trusted friends and family members thought of you and this woman together.

Treat your date like she's your friend because the best foundation for marriage is friendship. Even as your relationship progresses, always work on your friendship with this person. This means both of you will be able to be yourselves, honest, see the other person unselfishly, have fun, do things with other people, have similar interests, and feel your connection at a heart level as well as intellectually.

Obviously, physical attraction is important, but it doesn't hold up when it's the main focus or driving force of your interest in this person. Instead, these are the important elements that build a deep friendship and a stable, healthy dating relationship: inner beauty, emotional and spiritual connection, similar passions, being able to communicate well, ability to resolve conflicts, having fun, going on adventures, being at peace, and respecting one another.

15. Red Flags, Bells, and Whistles

Activation

When I had that week-long break from Brenda, I valued my parents and what they said to me. They were sounding boards for me, and I made myself accountable to them. For the most part, they basically just listened and repeated back to me what I was telling them, so I could see it more clearly. I valued and respected their blessing on my marriage, and I valued their input. I wanted to make sure I was marrying someone I really did want to spend the rest of my life with.

How many of your friends and family members have gotten divorced because they didn't pay attention to the red flags? They swept them under the carpet and later had the rug pulled right out from under them.

If your parents are in that category, have you fully forgiven them for the way their marriage went? Have you forgiven them for their divorce? Have you vowed never to be like them? Remember, making a vow not to be like someone causes us to focus on the very thing we're trying to avoid. Anything we haven't forgiven will end up hurting us, and there is a high chance that we will do exactly what we have vowed not to do.

So if you haven't done so, forgive your parents for their failed marriage and choose not to hold a grudge against them. Focus on what you *will* do, not on what you will not do.

Father, help me be true to myself and not be caught up in the bells and whistles of being in a relationship. I want to seek Your security and comfort and not place all my hope in a relationship. Please give me courage to take risks and do what I know I need to do. Please bless my relationships and bring me community. If anything is hidden, please bring it to the surface so it can connect with the truth of Jesus. May I be able to be vulnerable in my relationships and honor and respect my friends. Pour Your value for life into me so I can honor the people around me and the gift and sanctity of marriage. Thank You for giving me the freedom to choose. Amen.

Single LifeTip

I wouldn't have met my wife if I hadn't agreed to go with some friends to an event I didn't really want to go to. I think they pretty much dragged me to it. So, yeah. Get out. Do things you might not really want to. There is plenty of time to sit around and watch Netflix—like every day when you're married.

— Joey

15. Red Flags, Bells, and Whistles

16

The Ending That Begins

When I moved to Redding, I decided to focus on building friendships with women instead of trying to date right away. Two months after my move, my friendship circle expanded a little more to include a woman named Melissa.

When I met her, right away I thought highly of her. I could see she had a lot of character and that she was strong, beautiful, friendly, and impressive. In the beginning, I didn't get to interact with her very much because I could sense she wasn't open to it, so I gave her space. However, when it worked out, I would stop and talk with her. Sometimes we'd end up at the same parties or find ourselves around each other at other events, and we'd have some good laughs, share about each other, and catch up.

After I'd lived in Redding for a while, I started asking girls out on dates and had some great times. But nothing went past a second date, and plenty of "I just want to be friends" passed back and forth between these women and me.

Melissa and I had been friends for almost a year when she went back home for the summer after her first year of ministry school. She decided to return for the second year of schooling, which was great news for me. When I learned of a benefit dinner concert featuring Sean Feucht, I wanted to go and immediately thought of the woman I wanted to take with me. My friend Melissa.

16. The Ending That Begins

So I drove over to her house. She wasn't there, but I knew all her housemates, so they let me in and I told them I wanted to ask Melissa to go to the concert with me. They helped me out by conveniently giving me her phone number, and I texted to let her know I had a question for her.

When she returned a short time later, I asked her to the concert—in front of her housemates. Luckily, she said yes.

A few weeks later when we attended the benefit, the evening was a bit awkward. I know I was a little uptight because this was new and she was my friend, and I thought maybe she felt that way too. To take my mind off things, I focused on the reason we were there—to benefit others—and on worship during the worship time.

In the weeks following, Melissa and I went on walks occasionally. About a month after our first date, I took her to the Sundial Bridge, one of Redding's key landmarks, and as we walked, we shared a lot more about each other. I took her to dinner that evening, and on our way to the restaurant, I came up with the courage to tell her I wanted to pursue her in a dating relationship. I wanted to make sure she knew that I was interested in her and that I had a purpose in spending time with her. I wasn't just looking to have a good time.

"I would like to get to know you more," she replied, "but not dating."

That, obviously, was not the answer I wanted, but I understood it was where she was at the moment. For me, we'd been friends for over a year and I was fine with dating. At our table in the restaurant, we continued our conversation and we had fun together. I told her that I was fine with just being friends and that I would ask other girls out.

"If something changes, I will let you know," she said.

I trusted her. I knew she had lots of character, that her friends and mine highly respected her, and that she carried herself well and dressed modestly. I was impressed with her eight-plus years of being a missionary and now she was a second-year student at the Bethel school. She was funny and witty, a good listener, and I really thought she was pretty.

That was a Friday. On Sunday after church, we had lunch together. We talked about what it looks like to be friends, and we discussed our dating history. I wanted her to be comfortable being nice to me, and I made sure she knew I wasn't going to read anything into it and automatically start thinking she had changed her mind. I wanted to be nice to her in return and for it not to feel manipulative to her, like I was trying to get her to like me. If or when Melissa decided she was interested in dating, she could tell me directly and clearly.

This arrangement took all the pressure off of her, and we got everything out in the open, which was really, really helpful. She was able to relax around me more.

Her birthday is at the end of January, and at her party, there was no doubt that we enjoyed each other's company. It was there that I saw the first glimpse of maybe. Maybe she was changing her mind about me. On her actual birthday a few days later, I got her a small bouquet of flowers, placed them on her front patio, and texted that there was a surprise for her.

Yes, I took a risk getting flowers for my friend, but I wanted to celebrate her and express my value for our friendship. I knew she would enjoy the flowers, and at this point, I wasn't afraid of any criticism from her because we trusted each other. Our friendship was real, and I wasn't trying to impress her. It wasn't about me looking good or trying to force my hand; it was purely about celebrating my friend.

The following week, we played pool together and I had a great time. We laughed—there was a lot of laughter—and I started thinking that if we could have this much fun playing pool, on top of the friendship we had carefully built, then perhaps something might be going on between us.

That Sunday after we sat together in church, I took her fishing up at Lake Shasta. She had gotten her one-day fishing pass, and we spent the day together at the lake. Afterward, we put our equipment away and took a walk to another part of the lake.

As we were looking at the tree line and the blue sky on that warm day at the end of January, Melissa told me that things had changed. She informed me that I'd done a very good job of pursuing her, and I welcomed the opportunity to date her. On our walk back to the car, we decided we would be exclusive. We didn't catch any fish that day, but we caught each other! (Sorry/not sorry for the dad joke there.)

Everything I did in an attempt to set her at ease and get to know her without any pressure changed her heart toward me. My story ended up being exactly what I wanted—I wanted to be friends with a woman for a while before we started dating, so there was already trust built between us, no reason for pressure, and very little awkwardness.

When She Said Yes

One day while I was working on this book at Madayne, a local coffee shop, I decided to ask the two girls sitting at a nearby table an impromptu question: What would they say to my readers?

After we'd talked for a few minutes, one of the girls, Andi, told me, "I have a full life by myself. I am not waiting on someone to do something with. I am drawn towards people that are like that." She knows a lot of people who do "easy" things while dating, like going out to eat, getting drinks, or going to the movies. But she wisely thought it would be better for people to do something that improved their lives, something challenging, like developing a hobby or a skill.

Andi also shared that she hates dating books that are written from someone who has a success story at the end.

Well. There's not much I can do about that, at this point.

Melissa is from Australia, and she had to return to her country this summer because she was in the States on a student visa. After dating for five months, we knew that we wanted to spend

16. The Ending That Begins

the rest of our lives together. I wanted to marry her and she wanted to marry me.

So I flew over to see her, arriving in Melissa's small country town near the outback. The ring had been carefully brought over with me, and that first day, right after breakfast, I told her dad, "I'd like to see your shop out back."

He gave me a big, knowing smile and was delighted when I privately asked him for permission to marry his daughter.

After lunch, I told Melissa that I would like to see Charters Towers, a small town known for its massive gold rush in the 1850s. She didn't think anything of this request because she knew that I wanted to go to the top of Towers Hill, the historical site of the gold rush and the only place high enough to offer a great view of the area. She also knew that her sister Wendy and I had gone somewhere together to look at proposal sights, but she wasn't 100 percent sure that Towers Hill was one of them.

It totally was. Wendy and I had scoped the place out and planned where she would hide and take photos.

So that afternoon, Melissa and I drove to the top of the hill, and I led her over to a boulder that was off the trail about fifty feet. It was the best spot I could see and overlooked the countryside. I tried to recite a poem of sorts to her, but I couldn't remember exactly what I had written because I was nervous. So I improvised, all the while beaming with joy and excitement, and got down on my knees and asked Melissa, my adorable girlfriend, to marry me.

And what do you know? She said yes!

(Just a side note here, because I can't help myself: I am so blessed to be with you, Melissa. I love you with all my heart and everything that I am, and I am looking forward to being your husband and sharing all of me with you, for the rest of my life. Okay. Back to the rest of the book.)

When I think back over the journey of writing this book, I am amazed at what God has done. I started this book two years ago, at a time when I was very single. But then I met Melissa; I became her friend, dated her, and now, at long last, we both get to see the fulfillment of hope.

What Now?

Where does this leave you? What are you going to do?

Now that you have read this book, what things are you going to get involved in? What relationships are you going to focus on? How are you going to take care of your heart and process your pain? Who are you going to partner with, so you can walk through the single life with excellent friends?

As you take risks and pursue your hopes and dreams, this is my prayer for you:

> *Father God, thank You that we are not defined by how things look in our lives or where we are in life. Thank You for being with us during the process of growth and for making us holy and*

pure. I pray that the man reading this prayer will be able to remember how to love himself each day and to receive Your love for him, which will bring him peace like nothing else.

I pray for life to the fullest for him. And if he feels like this is too much to grasp right now, I pray that he would have a healthy life and the ability and experience to enjoy the man You made him to be. I pray that light would be brought to every secret area of pain and that he would have a friend or two who would help carry his burdens for him. I pray that he would find fun hobbies that bring him freedom and excitement, that would touch his heart and give him what he needs.

I pray that he would meet amazing people and grow in his ability to talk to the opposite sex. I pray for protection over his heart as he does these things and that he would know he is loved so much that he wouldn't need to build walls over his heart to protect it. I pray that he would be able to receive love, listen to others, and see them as actual people, just like he is.

I pray for healing in his family, for good communication, and that every awkward or painful thing would be healed and discussed fully.

I pray for favor for him at work or in his career. For an awareness of what he wants to do for work. For the courage to go after what he wants to do and to pursue more schooling or training if that is required. To quit his job and get a better one. To ask himself the difficult questions that lead to a greater career or opportunities that are a better fit.

I pray that this man would have fun times and adventures! That he would be able to travel, even to the close-by places that he hasn't gone to yet. I pray that he would have courage to step out. To have an event or invite others to an event. To host a game night or worship night. To get outdoors and do something he hasn't done before. To see the world. To plan for it.

I pray a blessing on his finances and on his ability to steward what he has well, so that he can have more and be able to enjoy it. That he would live within his means and be mindful of saving—but that he would also be able to enjoy the moment.

I pray blessing on his time. That it would not be wasted but enjoyed. That he would be able to enjoy the beauty around him, including himself. That he would discover who he is and who he is called to be. That his time is rich.

I pray for hope for this man. That no matter where he is in life, that he would believe that You are good and that he is loved perfectly. That his hope would be in You and not in himself. That he would be able to be thankful for all the gifts of life.

I pray for healing for his heart. For the courage to stay in the pain instead of medicating it with food, porn, being busy, movies, video games, work, etc. I pray that he would learn and remember what he needs and how good it feels to turn to healthy outlets. And I pray he would be able to stay in the pain and really feel again. No more numbing.

God, thank You for loving us so dearly and for being with us. Thank You for everyone in our lives and that we are significant no matter what. That our value is in what You think about us. We are Yours and everything we have is Yours. Thank You that we can partner with You and that You are in us and not some far-off God or deity. Thank You that we can partner with You in loving others, because we are so well loved by You ourselves.

Thank You, Father, for hearing my prayers. Thank you that the man reading this prayer today doesn't need to be afraid of being single, that it is okay to be single and not to be involved with anyone right now. And thank you for giving him the courage to ask the girl out that he wants to.

Thank You for Your presence. Bless this reader in every way. Amen.

Ask Her Out

Bibliography

Backlund, Steve, Jaramillo, Kim, Alhindi, Ahab, Smith, Melissa, Stevenson, Katrina. *Declarations: Unlocking Your Future.* Redding, CA: Igniting Hope Ministries, 2013.

Backlund, Wendy. *Victorious Emotions: Creating a Framework for a Happier You.* Redding, CA: Steve Backlund, 2017.

Eldredge, John. *Wild at Heart: Discovering the Secret of a Man's Soul.* Nashville: Thomas Nelson, 2001.

Eldredge, John and Stasi. *Captivating: Unveiling the Mystery of a Woman's Soul.* Nashville: Thomas Nelson, 2005.

Goff, Abram. "How to Ask a Girl Out." Moral Revolution. https://moralrevolution.com/how-to-ask-a-girl-out/.

Suggested Resources

Here is a list of resources that have helped me that I want you to share.

For growing in relationship and communication skills:

"Keep your love on" by Danny Silk.

"Love and Respect" by Dr. Eggerichs.

"Boundaries" by Cloud and Townsend.

"Telling yourself the truth" by William Backus and Marie Chapian.

Single Life Workshop, or e- course by Nothing Hidden Ministries Barry and Lori Burne. You can purchase the e course and turn it into a home group.

For growing as a man:

Imanalive.com- Join an online group or start a men's group of your own.

Watch the movie "Cinderella Man", "Pursuit of Happyness" "Braveheart" and "Gladiator". "The Man from Snowy River" "Rudy", "The Shack". What are some movies you have watched that inspire you to be a better man?

Read the book, "Discovering The Mind of a Woman", by Ken Nair.

"Wild at Heart" by John Eldredge.

"What Color is Your Parachute?"

Material that has especially made an impact for my spiritual growth:

"Who Do you think you are?" By Ray Leight.

"Ragamuffin Gospel" by Brennan Manning.

"Experiencing the Impossible" by Bill Johnson.

"Culture of Honor" by Danny Silk.

"Declarations" by Steve Backlund.

"Intercessory prayer" by Dutch Sheets.

"Birthing the Impossible" by Heidi Baker.

"Draw the Circle" by Mark Batterson

"The Divine Romance. 365 Days Meditating on the Song of Songs by Brian Simmons and Gretchen Rodriquez.

Sexuality resources:

Freedomu.net

Moralrevolution.com

Imanalive.com

Acknowledgments

Dad, thank you for being there for me. For being open and approachable. For sharing with me your mistakes and how you learned from them, how you succeeded in growing in communicating with Mom and learning how to be a servant leader. You've been an excellent example of perseverance as an electrical engineer, passing your exams to be certified throughout the nation and abroad. Thank you for spending time with me while I was growing up—riding bikes, going on hikes, bowling, and praying with me, and as an adult sharing life together.

Thank you for loving my mom and all of us so well and for celebrating fifty years of marriage in 2017. I love you, Dad.

Melissa, Thank you with all of my heart for responding with a yes to my pursuit of you. This has without a doubt been the best year of my life! I love you heaps! Thank you for your love, sweetness, friendship and encouragement. I could write another entire book on our fun and meaningful experiences this past year...maybe I will!

Made in the USA
San Bernardino, CA
11 January 2019